Innovation in South Gate

A Framework for Restructuring City Government

Brent R. Keltner
Ellen M. Pint
Eugene Bryton
Cathy S. Krop
Robert Reichardt
William L. Spencer
Suzanne Perry

*Prepared for the
City of South Gate*

RAND

This report documents findings from a management and organizational evaluation for the City of South Gate. In conducting the evaluation, RAND's goal is to help the city maintain a high level of performance in an increasingly dynamic political and economic environment. The report offers a series of recommendations for improving the city's ability to conduct strategic planning, to generate revenue, to streamline internal operations, and to improve resource management.

Research for the report was conducted over a three-month period beginning in the middle of March 1996 and continuing into the middle of June 1996. Our research efforts included interviews with the City Council, city staff, and city residents; a review of relevant city documents; consultation with in-house RAND experts; contact with innovative city governments throughout the United States and Canada; and a review of the literature on innovation in public- and private-sector organizations. Work on the evaluation was conducted within RAND's Domestic Research Division.

The management and organizational evaluation was commissioned by South Gate's City Council. The council specifically wanted RAND to help the city

- Maintain its current high standards of quality in operations and service levels;

- "Work smarter" by identifying areas where improvements and enhanced efficiencies can occur;

- Streamline operations and consolidate structural functions;
- Enhance responsiveness to the diverse constituency it serves; and
- Identify ways to improve fiscal practices.

Although the report is directed mainly at the City of South Gate, it will also be used as an input into further RAND research on local and municipal governments. The report is a first attempt to create a framework for understanding the issues related to restructuring city governments. Other cities should be able to draw on elements of the framework to critically analyze their own operations.

CONTENTS

FIGURES

TABLES

South Gate has a history of well-performing and responsive city government. Following the loss of high-paying manufacturing jobs in the early 1980s, city leaders moved quickly to respond to emerging economic realities by working with business and community groups to update the city's General Plan. Faced with revenue shortfalls, the city has moved to cut costs and to look for ways to improve revenue generation. The city's efforts to more fully integrate minorities and youths within the community have been recognized with the award of the National Civic League's "All-American City Award." The success of Community Oriented Policing and other community-outreach programs has led to high citizen approval ratings for the city's Police Department.[1]

Although the city has done well historically, it has not yet fully embraced the new and more volatile environment confronting municipalities throughout the country. Like other city governments, the City of South Gate must embrace a range of dramatic changes in its political, demographic, and economic environment. The city at present faces three broad challenges. The first is to maintain adequate service levels at a time when the city's resource base is shrinking and demand for city services is expanding. Adjusting for inflation, South Gate's general revenues have remained flat since 1986.[2] Flat revenues normally mean that a city can neither increase the level of services offered nor make the needed investments (in training and technology, for example) to improve the quality of

---

[1] In a 1996 survey of citizen satisfaction with their Police Departments conducted by faculty and students of Cal State Fullerton, South Gate ranked 11th among the 75 Los Angeles cities surveyed and 2nd among cities in its immediate region.

[2] See the discussion in Chapter Four.

service delivery. In South Gate's case, revenues have remained flat at a time of dynamic population growth. Between 1986 and 1996, the number of residents in South Gate increased by 19 percent, from 77,500 to 92,000.[3] The combination of flat revenues and population increases has put pressure on the city to provide even basic services.

The second broad challenge to the city and city staff is governing in a divided community. The South Gate community has at least three significant divisions. To begin with, the main business associations have not historically worked well together. As characterized by members of the business community themselves, there has been little cooperation or interaction between the Chamber of Commerce, the Tweedy Mile Association, and the Firestone Business Association, among others. In addition, there are also divisions between South Gate's business community and South Gate residents who are fearful of business development efforts.

A final important division runs along cultural and ethnic lines. The dramatic population growth of the last decade coincided with a shift toward an overwhelmingly Latino population. Between 1980 and 1996, the city's Latino population increased from 58 percent to 87 percent of the total city population. Although the city has made important first steps toward integrating the Latino population, this dramatic demographic change has not been fully embraced within the community or City Hall. Community divisions like these, which are not unique to South Gate, complicate municipal governance. In developing an agenda for a community, considerable time and resources can be wasted arbitrating between different interest groups.

A third challenge being faced by the city government is the growing expectations of business owners and residents of higher levels of responsiveness, cost-effectiveness, and quality. At all levels of government, citizens are expecting government bodies to do more with fewer resources. Residents of South Gate, like residents of other communities, want increased input into decisions about the city's resource allocation. As taxpayers, they want to be assured that the city government is doing things as cost effectively as possible. As consumers, city residents have grown accustomed to high levels of

---

[3]These are the official statistics published by the California Department of Finance. Unofficial estimates by city leaders put the figure at closer to 100,000.

quality and responsiveness from their private-sector service providers. They expect the city government to provide the same high level of service.

To meet these emerging challenges, the city will need to improve its overall operations and management in a number of ways. It will need to improve its ability to solicit input and build consensus within the community. It will need to improve its capacity for establishing priorities and for aligning internal resources to meet these priorities. It will need to more actively address the issue of revenue generation. It will also need to improve internal coordination between departments and to realize operational efficiencies to reduce resource requirements.

This report makes a series of recommendations that should help improve the city's abilities to achieve each of these goals. Our recommendations are organized into the following categories: strategic planning and internal resource alignment, planning revenue streams and core competencies, internal operations and service delivery, and managing common resources. Our recommendations are summarized below.

STRATEGIC PLANNING AND INTERNAL RESOURCE ALIGNMENT

Strategic planning can be an effective tool in dealing with many of the challenges currently faced by the City of South Gate. It can help to solicit input and overcome divisions within the community. It can help the city achieve better customer focus and improved resource allocation by more clearly setting goals and priorities. It can also help the city achieve internal resource alignment. In the area of strategic planning, we recommend that the city

- Initiate a year-long, participatory strategic planning process to set goals and priorities for the city over the next five to ten years;

- Revisit goals for manufacturing, retail, and housing development set in 1984;

- Work with business and community groups to create a clear "vision" for land use and economic development in the city;

- Use the strategic planning process to work toward alignment of internal resources by creating a schedule of development and infrastructural projects and a long-term budget; and

- Improve resource alignment by creating Common Resource Planning Teams to assist with strategic and operational planning in the areas of information technology, fiscal and budget practices, human resource management, and communications.

PLANNING REVENUE STREAMS AND CORE COMPETENCIES

Revenue planning needs to be much more clearly linked to the city's core competence and values. The strategic planning process should help the city identify its core sources of competitive advantage and core value commitments. These, in turn, need to guide and inform a plan for improving revenue streams. In the area of revenue generation, we recommend that the city

- Improve revenue generation from land use by linking development policy more closely to the city's core competencies;

- Enlist the support of business and community groups in putting the city's "vision" for economic development and land use into operation;

- Use city goals and values to guide an annual review of fees and fines;

- Support a review of fees and fines by making an annual review of costs part of the budget cycle;

- Expand efforts to sell and contract services by more clearly linking city activities to core competencies;

- Consider selling Public Works services where the city has a competitive advantage and contracting for services where it is less cost competitive; and

- Create a grant coordinator position to help city departments identify and pursue grant opportunities that fit well with their core competencies.

INTERNAL OPERATIONS AND SERVICE DELIVERY

Strategic planning and defining core competencies and values can help the city both to build consensus and to improve revenue generation. Efficiency gains and improvements in customer service, however, can be realized only through more careful attention to internal operations. Streamlining internal operations will not only lead to more cost-effective service delivery but will also improve quality to customers. In the area of internal operations, we recommend that the city

- Establish a Housing Division within the Community Development Department;

- Create a Public Information Office responsible for overseeing and coordinating all contact with citizens and business in South Gate;

- Shift employees out of the City Clerk's Office to the Public Information Office;

- Create a cross-functional process improvement team to redesign job processes related to opening a new business;

- Transfer full authority for technology planning and implementation to the Common Resource Planning Team for information technology;

- Form "contracting" teams of managers and employees to make decisions about selling and contracting for city services;

- Streamline the process of opening a new business by creating a full-case-manager approach to service delivery, an on-line database linking departments and divisions, and clear performance measures for all stages in the process;

- Streamline procurement by creating an on-line procurement database to link departments and divisions and by introducing performance measurements for key steps in the procurement process;

- Set up a process to pay vendors up front or use partial payments to allow the city to negotiate lower prices on purchased goods and materials;

- Link business process improvement efforts to technology policy and human resource management; and

- Implement Monday through Thursday staffing in all employment positions, but consider providing "time-sensitive" services on Fridays.

MANAGING COMMON RESOURCES

The city's ability to realize its strategic goals and to realize improved efficiencies in day-to-day operations depends upon how well it manages its common resources. In all city governments, departments need to manage a number of resources collectively. They include information technology, budget and finances, human resources, and communications. To improve coordination between departments and to support the diffusion of innovative ideas, South Gate needs a more systematic approach to resource management in each of these areas. In the area of common resource management resources, we recommend that the city

- Use Common Resource Planning Teams to plan operational management of information technology, fiscal and budget practices, human resource management, and communications;

- Develop a strategic plan and an implementation plan for the city's information technology infrastructure before finalizing a request for proposal (RFP) to technology vendors;

- Develop a cross-departmental plan for using information technology to support business process improvement and performance measurement efforts;

- Develop an explicit policy on fund transfers and consider lowering the present authorization level;

- Develop better oversight of investment responsibilities by making the Finance Director deputy to the City Treasurer on all investment policy;

- Consolidate all financial management responsibilities within the Finance Department;

- Improve coordination of all activities related to risk management by creating a formal role for the risk management committee;

- Redesign performance evaluations and encourage increased cross-department skill formation;

- Create a new performance-based compensation system that integrates both broad-banding and competency-based pay;

- Develop a "new" employment contract, detailing employee responsibilities and conditions for employment security;

- Introduce a self-service delivery system for internal documents and reports and a system of contact persons for new employees in each department to facilitate internal communication; and

- Revise the customer satisfaction survey and create a common marketing strategy with key stakeholders in the community to improve external communications.

The report's recommendations are based on a wide variety of data-collection efforts. These include interviews with the City Council, city staff, and city residents; a review of relevant city documents; consultation with in-house RAND experts; contacts with innovative city governments throughout the United States and Canada; and a review of the literature on innovation in public- and private-sector organizations.

ACKNOWLEDGMENTS

Completing this report would not have been possible without the help and assistance of many people. We would like to thank foremost Ed Edelman and David Kassing of RAND. Both acted as senior advisers to the project and played an important role in getting the research team off to a strong start. Xandra Kayden of the UCLA Public Policy School and Susan Gates of RAND provided thoughtful and constructive reviews of an earlier version of this document. Comments from both reviewers strengthened our analysis, though the authors bear full responsibility for the final product. Within the City of South Gate, the City Manager and department heads gave us invaluable support in completing our project. They were generous with their time and made sure we had access to all necessary records and documents. City employees had many thoughtful and insightful suggestions, which aided our research. Finally, we owe a specail debt of gratitude to Maren Manlowe, Patricia Bedrosian, and Christina Pitcher. By so effectively coordinating meetings within South Gate, Maren contributed greatly to the smooth progression of the project. At RAND, Patricia Bedrosian and Christina Pitcher both worked diligently and efficiently to make sure we met our publication deadlines.

Chapter One

INTRODUCTION AND RESEARCH APPROACH

The demands being placed on municipal governments have increased dramatically over the past several years. Downsizing in state and federal government agencies has forced cities to assume a greater burden of service delivery in many areas. Declining resource streams are increasing demands on efficiency. Higher consumer expectations of quality along with the growing diversity of many urban communities are placing greater demands on cities' responsiveness to their constituents. Although these new political and economic circumstances are making municipal governance more difficult, a variety of organizational and technological innovations are improving cities' ability to cope with this more demanding environment.

Cities that are prospering in this new environment are those that have made a commitment to transforming themselves by adopting many of the management and organizational techniques found in high-performing private-sector organizations. These include strategic planning, a commitment to process redesign and performance measurement, teaming and teamwork, effective use of information technology, and employee involvement and employee empowerment. The City of South Gate has made some first, innovative steps in many of these areas, but it still has a long way to go to fully realize the potential of these new organizational techniques. RAND's goal in conducting this management and organizational evaluation is to speed the process of innovation by combining a deep understanding of issues faced by the City of South Gate with state-of-the-art knowledge on organizational practice.

RESEARCH FRAMEWORK

RAND's approach to the management and organizational evaluation was heavily influenced by the literature on high-performing organizations. Both public- and private-sector organizations have begun to implement a number of management innovations to improve the quality and cost-effectiveness of service delivery. Our research framework was based on investigating how far South Gate had moved in implementing high-performance strategies in five areas. These included

- *Strategic planning.* High-performance organizations are using creative, exploratory strategic planning to establish goals, define their core mission, and identify core sources of competitive advantage.[1]

- *Process redesign and performance measurement.* Innovative organizations are using process redesign and performance measurement to systematically track and modify the way core work processes are organized. Process redesign can be used to continuously reduce costs, improve quality, and increase customer satisfaction.[2]

- *Teaming and teamwork.* In high-performance organizations, cross-functional and cross-departmental teams are used to speed and improve decisionmaking. Teams are composed of individuals with complementary skills, shared goals, and mutual accountability.[3]

- *Effective use of information technology.* Innovative organizations are using information technology to support improved information sharing, customer service, process redesign, and performance measurement.[4]

- *Employee involvement and employee empowerment.* High-performing organizations are giving more attention to employees as a critical input into production. They are using employee in-

---

[1]See Hamel and Prahalad (1994) and Fombrun (1994).

[2]See Hammer and Champy (1993) and Camp (1989).

[3]See Katzenback and Smith (1993) and Mohrman, Cohen, and Mohrman, Jr. (1995)

[4]See Davenport (1993) and Gore (1993).

volvement programs, improved incentives, and redesigned training to better harness the employee as a resource.[5]

Drawing on the literature about high-performance organizations, we were able to address most but not all of the issues presented in the City of South Gate's Request for Proposals. Two elements of the RFP which did not fit easily into our framework were the requests for

- An analysis of the city's financial philosophy and budgeting; and

- An evaluation of four- versus five-day city operations.

We added these two issues as further parts of the research framework. With these five elements of our research framework and two specific research tasks, we began the process of evaluating South Gate's management, organization, and fiscal practices.

DATA COLLECTION

Research for the project involved the use of four complementary data-collection techniques (see Table 1). The first was a large number of interviews and meetings with individuals both within City Hall and in the South Gate community. Within City Hall, meetings were conducted with individual members of the City Council, department heads, the City Manager, and employees in all of the departments. Within the South Gate community, interviews were conducted with business owners and business associations, community and citizen groups, real estate agents, and developers.[6] As part of the study we also reviewed a large number of city documents. These included budgets, organization charts, annual reports, policies and procedures manuals, minutes of City Council meetings, records on city contracts, financial management plans, and documentation on staffing and job design.

A third type of data collection was a review of innovative practices in other cities. In the course of our research, we contacted a large number of cities to discuss strategic planning, budgeting and fiscal

---

[5]See Pfeffer (1994) and Blinder (1990).

[6]A list of the business and community groups we met with is in Appendix A.

management, use of information technology, and human resource management. Finally, to gather more information about innovative organizational practices, we consulted with a number of in-house RAND experts. RAND researchers were contacted to gather information on issues related to planning and implementing information technology systems, on survey research techniques, and on process redesign and measurement techniques.

Table 1

An Overview of Data Collection

Technique	Sources of Information	Areas of Research Framework Covered
Interviews in South Gate	City Council and city staff Business owners and associations Community and civic groups Real estate agents and developers	All
City document review	Budgets Organization charts, Annual reports Policies and procedures manuals Minutes of City Council meetings Records on city contracts Documents on staffing and job design	All
Contacts in other cities	31 cities	Strategic planning Budgeting and financial management Use of information technology Human resource management
Expert interviews	RAND researchers	Implementation of information technology systems Business process improvement Survey research techniques

SELECTION AND ORGANIZATION OF RECOMMENDATIONS

Following our data collection and analysis, we developed a series of recommendations for changes and improvements. These recommendations were integrated into a draft report that was circulated to the City Manager and the city's department heads for feedback on the accuracy of findings and on the feasibility of implementing our recommendations. Feedback from these individuals was then incorporated into the final version of the report.

The ordering of our recommendations mirrors the logic of how we thought through the problem of restructuring the city government. The recommendations begin with strategic planning and planning revenue streams, move to internal operations and service delivery, and finish with resource management issues.[7] Both strategic planning and planning revenue streams are part of the process of definining key goals, competencies, and values. Both activities are integral to answering the questions "what is the organization's core mission" and "what are the organization's core competencies." The chapter on planning revenue streams could easily have been subsumed in the one on strategic planning. But, given the importance of revenue generation to South Gate and the length of our recommendations in this area, we decided to make it a separate chapter.

Once an organization has completed its strategic planning and planning revenue streams, the next set of decisions that must be taken relate to internal operations and service delivery. The goal of this phase of decisionmaking is to create structures and work processes that help an organization most effectively realize its goals. Decisions on structure and process create the context for the organization's operations. The final set of decisions relate to resource management. Having decided upon structure and process, an organization needs to establish policies that allow for effective, ongoing management of financial, technological, and human resources as well as communications. Policies and procedures for managing these four common resource areas should ensure smooth day-to-day operations.

---

[7]The logic behind the organization of our recommendations parallels that used in earlier RAND work that relied on a "strategy-to-tasks" framework for guiding the restructuring of military organizations. See Lewis, Coggin, and Roll (1994).

Chapter Two

STRATEGIC PLANNING AND INTERNAL RESOURCE ALIGNMENT

A first area for findings and recommendations relates to strategic planning. Leaders of private-sector companies have formally used strategic planning to improve organizational performance at least since the mid-1960s. The basic goal of a strategic plan is to create an overall vision for an organization's future. Private-sector managers have used strategic planning to articulate core commitments and competencies, outline challenges, and set goals for the years ahead. Strategic planning has also been used to achieve better internal resource alignment. By clearly setting goals and priorities, strategic planning is a first step in making decisions about resource commitments.

With the shift toward putting government operations on a more business-like footing, strategic planning is now becoming increasingly important to public-sector organizations. A commitment to strategic planning has been institutionalized at the federal government level with the passing into law of the *Government Performance and Results Act* in 1993.[1] For city governments, there are no data available on how widespread strategic planning has become, but our interviews with both city officials and public- and private-sector consultants indicate that it is increasingly becoming a central element of municipal policymaking.

---

[1]The act requires that federal agencies submit a strategic plan by September 30, 1997, an annual performance plan for fiscal year 1999, and a performance report by March 31, 2000.

7

In the course of our research, we conducted interviews with officials in eight different municipalities that have initiated strategic planning processes (see Table 2).[2] Many of these cities had initiated participatory planning processes, with city officials involving citizen and community groups in the determination of goals and objectives. Interviews with officials in these eight municipalities suggest at least three benefits of participatory strategic planning:

- Reducing the politicization of major decisions by expanding the scope of participation;

- Encouraging more responsive and proactive government by clearly setting and signaling priorities; and

- Achieving alignment of internal resources with important goals and objectives.

South Gate's last major attempt at participatory strategic planning was in 1984, with the completion of the last General Plan. At present, the only true, ongoing strategic planning efforts take place under the rubric of the city's Youth Commission. The commission gives representatives of the city and community the opportunity to meet every other year to set goals and create policies for the city's youth. Participatory strategic planning needs to be extended to other key policy areas. We recommend that the City of South Gate initiate a one-year participatory strategic planning process that draws heavily on citizen input and focuses on creating goals and priorities for the city's development. Although key areas for further consideration must emerge from the planning process itself, our research and interviews suggest that economic development and land use policy should be a main focal point of planning. We also recommend that the planning process be used to work toward more effective internal resource alignment.

---

[2]The sample of cities contacted was selected to achieve a mix of small and large cities as well as cities with more and less ethnic diversity.

Table 2
An Overview of Eight Cities' Strategic Planning Processes

City	Name of Process (Year Initiated)	Main Focal Points of Planning Process	Key Participants
Culver City, CA	Direction 21 Process (1987)[a]	Create an overall vision for the community Rebuild downtown	City Council and staff Business and community leaders Citizens at large
Pasadena, CA	Community Growth Initiative (1991–1992)[b]	Community-supported plan for growth	City Council and staff Business and community leaders Citizens at large
Grand Prairie, Alberta	A Corporate Vision—City Council's Strategic Plan (1992–1993)	Economic development Improved use of technology Environmental policy	City Council and staff
Vancouver, British Columbia	CityPlan—Directions for Vancouver (1994–1995)	Downtown planning Housing development Internal operations	City Council and staff Business and community leaders Citizens at large
Monrovia, CA	Vision 2000 (1995)	Create a livable community Develop a vision for downtown	City Council and staff Business owners and business leaders
Charlotte, NC	Rightsizing in Charlotte (1993)	Internal restructuring Rightsizing Privatization	City Council and staff
Virginia Beach, VA	Destination Points for Virginia Beach (1993)[c]	Safe community Economic vitality	City Council and staff
Scottsdale, AZ	City Venture Team (1993) Community Visioning (1996)	Internal structure and operations Land use and urban design Circulation and transportation	City Council and staff Citizens at large

SOURCES: Interviews and city documents.

[a]Culver City is currently embarking on a second round of strategic planning.

[b]Pasadena completed a comprehensive strategic planning process in 1986. A second planning process was initiated in 1991 to look specifically at the question of community growth and development.

[c]Virginia Beach's City Council began setting annual goals in 1990. The annual goal-setting workshop was turned into a five-year plan in 1993.

PARTICIPATORY PLANNING

Planning for public-sector organizations is inherently more difficult than planning in the private sector.[3] Unlike private-sector planning, which may just involve managers or managers and employees, public-sector planning involves the coordination of a large number of stakeholders with diverse and often conflicting interests. In the case of a city government, key stakeholders will include city management and employees, the City Council, citizens, civic and community organizations, and business owners and associations. Because public-sector planning is about planning for the expenditure of "public" resources, it is also highly political. Together, these factors make it very easy for public-sector planning to degenerate into acrimony and partisanship.

To overcome barriers to public-sector planning, many innovative city governments are moving toward a participatory model of strategic planning. The central goal of participatory strategic planning is to depoliticize the process of setting goals and priorities. Participatory planning allows all key stakeholders to work together in setting a course for a city and in deciding how it will prioritize resource expenditures. City governments that have introduced participatory strategic planning are moving away from decisionmaking forums that contribute to divisiveness and polarization, e.g., public hearings, and toward those that promote consensus-building, e.g., small working groups and community workshops. By virtue of having the opportunity to participate in the planning process, all key stakeholders are more firmly bound to the final list of priorities. The participatory process is open and the final document is developed and agreed upon in public forums, which makes it difficult for a small group or faction to undercut the planning process.

In addition to minimizing politicization, the other main goal of participatory planning is to increase information flows within a city. By initiating a strategic planning process, a city government implicitly recognizes that many of the key resources for solving community problems lie within the community itself rather than within City Hall. In this new model of planning, the city's main role is to act as a

---

[3]For an overview of strategic planning in the public sector, see Blackerby (1994).

facilitator and consensus-builder—bringing diverse stakeholders to-gether to solve common problems. The participatory planning pro-cess can be used to increase the amount of feedback from commu-nity stakeholders to the city government, but it can also be used to encourage an improved dialogue between and among community stakeholders themselves. The planning process can, moreover, be used as a vehicle to support efforts by neighborhood, community, and business to better organize themselves.

To be successful, a participatory planning process must be preceded by what has been called a "plan-to-plan."[4] The plan-to-plan, which should be developed by city officials, describes the sequence of strategic planning and lists participants at each stage of the process. A variety of participatory techniques can be used by city govern-ments to involve community members in planning. They include advisory committees, workshops, speaker series and presentations, newsletters, and surveys (see Table 3). Each participatory technique has advantages and disadvantages and an associated cost. A city government needs to base the decision about which participatory techniques it will use on its own needs and the resources it has avail-able. It may also benefit from consulting professionals in the area of participatory planning.[5]

We feel that it is important for South Gate to make initiating a partic-ipatory strategic planning process one of its highest priorities for the coming year. As suggested in the summary to this report, a number of significant divisions exist within the city. These divisions have led to a number of false starts in the city's attempts to promote eco-nomic and municipal development. The controversy surrounding the attempt to build a bingo parlor is one example; the move to re-scind the State Street business district as a redevelopment area is another. The lack of a participatory approach to planning has also

---

[4]This term is used by Blackerby (1994, p. 18).

[5]As part of RAND's evaluation, the RAND project manager accompanied South Gate's Mayor and Deputy City Manager to a workshop on participatory planning. The work-shop was put on by the UCLA Extension Public Policy Program and featured presenta-tions from representatives of MIG, Inc., and Envicom. Both are consulting firms that have worked with governments throughout Southern California in developing partici-patory strategic planning processes.

Table 3

Public Participation Techniques and Participatory Planning Efforts in Southern California

Technique	Los Angeles	West Hollywood	San Clemente	Hunting-ton Beach	Redondo Beach	San Ber-nardino
Advisory committee		√	√	√	√	√
Workshops						
Citywide	√	√	√	√	√	√
Neighborhood	√	√				
Topic/issue		√				
Multi-day charrette	√					
Presentations						
Speaker forum	√	√				
Informal	√	√		√		
Media						
Cable TV						
Meetings	√	√			√	√
Panels	√	√		√		
Advertising	√	√	√	√		
Newspaper	√	√	√	√	√	√
Video/slide presentations	√					
Newsletters	√	√				√
Interviews/stakeholders	√	√				
Surveys/questionnaires		√				
Nontraditional outreach	√	√				
Estimated cost	$275K	$313K	$50K	$60K	$115K	$40K

SOURCE: Envicom, 1996 (prepared for the American Planning Association Orange County Section Nuts and Bolts Conference).

harmed the integrity of the political process, with some residents convinced that important decisions are driven more by political "log-rolling" than by what is best for the city.

For communities like South Gate with large minority and immigrant populations, investment in community-outreach efforts is a particularly important part of the planning process. To generate true consensus within the community, representatives of minority and recent immigrants need to have input into the planning process. These groups are, however, typically not well represented in the established community institutions and organizations and often are hard to reach. Soliciting information from these elements of the community often requires nontraditional outreach efforts. Interviews with city officials in communities with large Latino populations suggest that workshops conducted through schools, childcare centers, and the churches are the most effective way to reach this population segment.

SETTING AND SIGNALING PRIORITIES

A primary goal of strategic planning is to set, signal, and rank priorities in key policy areas. Setting and ranking priorities allow a city government to become a proactive rather than a reactive problem-solver. Many city officials we interviewed described their cities' operations before adopting a strategic plan as consumed by "putting out one fire after another." By adopting a strategic plan, they were able to increase confidence in the city government by giving citizens, community groups, and business leaders a clear sense of where the city planned to go over the coming years. The second advantage of outlining and ranking various strategic priorities is that it sends a strong signal to staff, City Council, and citizens about the limits of available resources. As one City Manager put it, clearly setting priorities allows city departments "to draw a red line on their list of activities and projects"—indicating how far available resources go in allowing them to accomplish these activities. If either the City Council or citizens want additional output from a department beyond the "red line," additional resources will need to be made available.

The issues to be addressed in South Gate's strategic plan must ultimately be established as part of the planning process itself. Although successful strategic planning ends with a coherent vision of an organization's future and a clear sense of goals and priorities, it should begin as an open-ended and creative process. Too often, strategic planning turns into strategic programming, with the process used to elaborate on strategies that already exist rather than to explore other possible worlds.[6] It would be imprudent and counterproductive for either RAND, as part of its analysis, or the city staff to allow the strategic planning process to begin with a preset agenda. Our research and interviews, however, do suggest that the issues related to economic development and land-use planning should be an important element of the planning process. Other issues that the city and community may want to address include capital improvement programs, additional youth programs, and circulation and transportation within the city.

ECONOMIC DEVELOPMENT AND LAND USE

The city last developed a comprehensive plan for economic development and land use in 1984. This plan, which was developed in consultation with business groups and South Gate residents, laid out a ten-year strategy for development and redevelopment within the city. Many of the objectives of this ten-year plan have been accomplished. Notable successes include the development of Tweedy Boulevard, especially the Tweedy Marketplace, and the partial redevelopment of the old General Motors site. Having accomplished many of the goals of the 1984 plan, it is now time for the city to address once again the issues of economic development and land use.

For this next strategic planning process and future planning efforts, we recommend that economic development goals be revisited more often than once every ten years or so. Although this planning horizon is well within the State of California's legal requirements for developing a General Plan, it is inadequate for cities such as South Gate, which have experienced dramatic economic and demographic changes. After developing comprehensive strategic plans, both Culver City and Pasadena revisited and updated their plans within seven to eight years. Within the broad category of economic development

---

[6]Mintzberg (1994).

and land use, three areas require specific attention. These are manufacturing development, retail development, and housing and neighborhood policy.

Manufacturing Development

During meetings with both community and business leaders, concerns were raised about the amount of industrial land that is either unused or underused. Underused land is not only unattractive but it hurts South Gate's tax base directly through loss of property taxes and through decreased employment opportunities for citizens. Many factors that affect industrial land use are beyond the control of a city government. The local real estate market is influenced by the health of the regional economy as well as by the objectives and desires of land owners and buyers. Moreover, the tools available to a city to influence redevelopment efforts are limited.[7] We feel that the city can make the best use of these tools and can help improve the use of industrial land by addressing the two following issues as part of the strategic planning process:

- *Identifying future growth industries*: Like a business, a city can develop a reputation for having a comparative advantage in certain types of economic activities. A clear reputation makes it easier to market the city and attract outside industries. As part of the strategic planning process, City of South Gate officials need to work with business and community groups to develop a clearer vision of South Gate's comparative advantage. Using available information,[8] community leaders need to identify future growth industries and create a plan for marketing the city to firms in these industries. At present, South Gate is not viewed by external industries as having any particular source of compara-

---

[7]The tools available to the city are discussed in Chapter Four.

[8]South East Los Angeles County (SELAC) has provided South Gate with information on the industry clusters that are the most promising growth areas for the city. In Appendix B, we have provided an analysis of South Gate's current employment patterns. Although information on recent industry entrance into and exit from South Gate would be most helpful in identifying future growth industries, information on present employment can be used to create a baseline.

tive advantage. Real estate agents we interviewed suggested that South Gate is often not the first place that business owners and managers think of when planning a new facility. Rather, South Gate tends to be considered after communities like Commerce and Vernon.

• *Addressing the issue of contaminated land*: Much of South Gate's undeveloped lands are Brownfield sites—old industrial properties that are unused because of concern about environmental contamination. Land owners resist selling Brownfield land for fear of being held financially accountable for cleanup efforts. Lenders are unwilling to lend money for the purchase and development of contaminated real estate. As a result, Brownfield sites often lie fallow for years to decades at a time, creating both an eyesore and lost revenues. There is little South Gate or any other city can do to force an owner to sell contaminated land or lenders to loan money for its development. In its role as a community facilitator, however, the city can use the strategic planning process to bring together land owners, industrialists, developers, and lenders to find common solutions to development hampered by contaminated land. The city should use the strategic planning process to create such a working group and to determine whether recent federal or state initiatives in this area can help the process of developing Brownfield sites (see Appendix C).

Retail Development

Sales and use taxes are the largest single source of general funds, representing over 25 percent of total general fund revenues. As shown in our revenue analysis (Chapter Three), sales and use taxes measured in nominal dollars have been flat since 1992. Measured in real dollars, sales tax receipts have been declining since 1988. The city and business community can improve prospects for retail development by prioritizing the two following issues during the strategic planning process:

• *Improving the mix of retail shops*: There are two ways to improve the mix of retail shops in South Gate. The first is by improving the cohesiveness of major retail districts. Developing a cohesive mix of shops in major retail districts, e.g., the Tweedy and Hollydale business districts, was an important priority and a main ac-complishment of the 1984 economic plan. Our own observa-tions, discussions with retailers, and discussions with city staff have led us to conclude that, over time and with the conclusion of the 1984 plan, the city's retail districts have become less cohe-sive. Other types of service providers (e.g., wholesalers, medical supply stores) have gradually become intermixed with retail es-tablishments. Less cohesive retail districts make South Gate a relatively less attractive area in which to shop.

The mix of retail shops can also be improved by better linking them to the current retail needs of South Gate residents. Anecdotal evidence suggests that there is a large outflow of retail revenues (and thus sales tax revenues for the city) from South Gate to other communities. Although a needs assessment was part of the 1984 plan, at present neither the business community nor the city has a clear understanding of purchasing patterns in the city.

As with manufacturing development, the city has a limited influ-ence on how the mix of retail shops within the city develops. Real estate agents typically have an incentive to move properties as quickly as possible, even when this may be in conflict with the city's desire to develop a cohesive mix of stores. Retail owners and retail associations, moreover, are better able to determine current purchasing patterns. They are closer to the market and have stronger incentives to survey and understand community retail needs. As part of the strategic planning process, the city needs to work with these groups and with residents and other large institutional consumers (e.g., the schools, large businesses) to continue to improve the current mix of retail stores.

- *Assisting start-up businesses:* Start-up businesses are important to the long-term viability of South Gate's retail infrastructure. With a low household income level relative to many other com-munities in Los Angeles,[9] the city will find it difficult to attract

---

[9]According to 1990 Census data, the median household income in South Gate was $27,279. Within Los Angeles County, the median household income was $34,965. The communities immediately surrounding South Gate had the following median in-comes: Paramount, $29,015; Bell Gardens, $23,819; Lynwood, $25,961; Maywood, $25,567; Lakewood, $44,700; Norwalk, $38,124; and Downey, $36,991.

many outside chains and franchises. This makes it particularly important for the city to nurture start-up enterprises. Recognizing the importance of start-ups to the city's overall economic development, both the city and local business groups have offered workshops and other events targeted at the small business owner. The Chamber of Commerce has offered free training workshops on how to set up a business, and the city has used its Business Fair as a way of reaching out to small businesses.

It is not clear in either case that these efforts are paying off. According to city staff, these events have not been well attended. There are a variety of possible explanations for the new business owners' lack of interest in the city and Chamber of Commerce's programs. They include unrealistic attitudes on the part of the new business owners (i.e., believing that they do not need help in starting a business), inadequate marketing on the part of the city, and cultural and linguistic barriers that impede communication. More important than assigning blame is that the city make it a priority as part of the strategic planning process to work with business organizations in identifying ways to reach the small business owner. The planning process should be used to combine city and business resources to create an environment more conducive to start-ups. The planning process should also be used to develop a strategy for supporting start-ups by new immigrants.[10]

Housing and Neighborhood Policy

An attractive and stable living environment is a very important element of overall municipal development. It is important to maintaining a sense of community and for recruiting new businesses into a

---

[10]Employees in City Hall and real estate owners in South Gate suggested that many of the conflicts and regulatory violations that occur are with businesses operated by immigrants who are not knowledgeable about the business environment in the United States. Discussions with the Center for Minority Youth Employment at Cal State Los Angeles suggest an apparent lack of targeted support in South Gate for small businesses started by immigrants. An example of an innovative program in this area in the City of Los Angeles is Charo's entrepreneurial training in both Spanish and English. This training focuses on giving students information needed in the real life operation of businesses, such as proper licensing and obeying signage regulations. The eleven-week classes cost about $1,700 per student and are paid for by the city government.

city. At present, South Gate has a high percentage of absentee owners, with just 50.3 percent of community residents both occupying
and owning a home. A typical figure in other more affluent communities is 60 to 65 percent. The large influx of recent immigrants
has also led to high levels of transience in the community. Although
a city government can do only so much to influence housing and
neighborhood development, the present lack of coordination within
City Hall on these issues has not helped create a more stable environment. A number of housing programs are being operated by the
city government, including ones targeting first-time homeowners
and low-income residents. These efforts, however, are dispersed and
uncoordinated. As part of the strategic planning process, the city
government should work with community residents and homeowners' associations to create a common housing and neighborhood
policy. The goal of planning should be to increase support for home
ownership and residential stability.

ALIGNING INTERNAL RESOURCES

The discussion of strategic planning to this point has addressed
working with community members and residents to create broad
goals and priorities. As part of the planning process, the city government also needs to create a mechanism to align internal resources with strategic priorities. At present, the city does not have
well-established procedures for planning and financing multiyear
tasks. It also does not have a clear strategy for managing internal resources.

Planning Development Projects

The strategic planning process can be expected to produce a large
number of possible community development and Public Works projects. To organize these projects into manageable tasks, the city
needs to create a multiyear implementation plan. The plan should
cover how the city plans to allocate financial resources and manpower to the different projects. The plan should, in addition, be used
to coordinate community and business resources within South Gate.
The city will not have sufficient manpower or funds available to support all possible projects. In its capacity as a facilitator, the city

should, however, be well placed to pull together resources from the diverse stakeholders in the community.

Creating a Long-Term Budget

To support multiyear projects, the city needs to develop a long-term budget. Currently, the city's planning process is dominated by the yearly budget cycle. The long-term budget should map out a three- to five-year plan for resource uses and requirements. This three- to five-year plan can be used to translate the strategic plan into one-year increments that can be incorporated into the yearly budget cycle. A long-term budget allows the city to look beyond yearly issues to plan and schedule the implementation of projects and processes that take longer than a year. The three- to five-year plan should be updated each year to allow for adjustment to new priorities and fiscal conditions.

The absence of a long-term budget has been a particularly vexing problem with regard to the development of the city's information infrastructure. Too often, systems and components are purchased in an uncoordinated or haphazard fashion using resources that are available only in one year's budget. It is particularly difficult to implement any systems or software that can be shared by more than one department. Under current procedures, software that benefits many departments will be considered only if one department takes the lead.

Creating Common Resource Planning Teams

To better align internal resources with strategic priorities, the city also needs to create Common Resource Planning Teams (CRPs). In a city government, all city departments draw upon and use four types of common resources in performing public services: (a) information technology, (b) financial resources and budgets, (c) human resources, and (d) internal and external communication. Recognizing the importance of appropriately managing common resources, many innovative cities have made "commons management" a central element of their overall strategic planning initiatives.[11] A systematic approach to managing common resources allows each city to improve coordination, avoid duplication, and support the diffusion of innovative ideas.

Both our own observations and comments made by city staff during interviews suggest that City of South Gate operations are at present heavily department-oriented. Informal networks have developed between employees to facilitate cross-departmental work but most of this contact occurs outside official channels. In addition, there are at present no mechanisms in place to share and coordinate innovative approaches to managing resources that affect all the city departments. To support increased cooperation across departments, we recommend that the city introduce Common Resource Planning Teams to advise and provide information to the departments and individuals responsible for managing common resources.

These teams should be composed of appropriately selected managers and employees from a range of city departments. They should provide feedback on both strategic and operational aspects of common resource planning. The ad hoc team on information technology has begun to play this role in the management of information technology. We recommend that the information technology team become a permanent part of the city's operation and that the city government move to establish teams in the areas of financial resource management, human resource management, and communications.

SUMMARY OF RECOMMENDATIONS ON STRATEGIC PLANNING AND INTERNAL RESOURCE ALIGNMENT

- Initiate a year-long, participatory strategic planning process to set goals and priorities for the city over the next five to ten years;

---

[11]Vancouver, British Columbia, wrote an independent plan to guide resource management in each of the four common resource areas. Virginia City, Virginia, has created Commons Policy Teams, comprising department directors and other middle managers, to offer advice and share ideas about the management of common resources. Virginia City has Commons Policy Teams in five areas—finance, technology, human resources, public relations, and buildings and land.

- Revisit goals for manufacturing, retail, and housing development set in 1984;

- Work with business and community groups to create a clear "vision" for land use and economic development in the city;

- Use the strategic planning process to work toward alignment of internal resources by creating a schedule of development and infrastructural projects and a long-term budget; and

- Improve resource alignment by creating Common Resource Planning Teams to assist with strategic and operational planning in the areas of information technology, fiscal and budget practices, human resource management, and communications.

PLANNING REVENUE STREAMS AND CORE COMPETENCIES

Declining revenue streams have been a problem for the City of South Gate for some time. Adjusting for inflation, South Gate's general fund revenues have remained flat since 1986 (Figure 1).[1] Had the city not increased internal reimbursement, i.e., drawn money from special funds to supplement the general fund, it would actually have experienced an overall decline in general fund revenues. Between 1989 and 1996, internal reimbursements increased by about $300,000 a year. The city has experienced declining general fund revenues in two main areas. The first is in sales and use taxes, which dropped from a high of $4,963,000 in 1988–1989 to a low of $3,653,846 in 1995–1996. The second is a drop in funds available from state and federal governments. Funds available from state and federal agencies, including the motor vehicle in-lieu transfer, declined by over $500,000 between 1986 and 1996.

Responding to these revenue losses, the city's staff has adopted a number of innovative revenue-generating schemes. These innovative strategies include increasing charges for police-related activities (e.g., vehicle impoundment, DUI billings), introducing a utility in-lieu tax on water, and increasing a range of user taxes and fees (e.g., transient occupancy tax, commercial refuse franchise, real estate transfers, and material recovery fees). Although these innovations

---

[1]Appendix D gives the raw data used in Figure 1. It gives data on both gross and adjusted revenues. We used the Council of Economic Advisors' deflators for state and local governments to make the inflation-adjusted calculation.

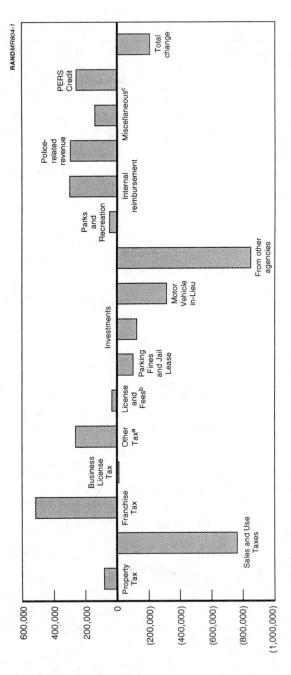

SOURCE: South Gate adopted budgets for fiscal years 1989/90, 1995/96.

NOTE: To reduce yearly fluctuations, revenues are averaged for two fiscal years.

aTransient Occupancy Tax, Commercial Refuse Franchise, Real Estate Transfer, Material Recovery Fee.

bBuilding, Electrical, and Other Permits; Plan Check; Animal License; Zoning fees.

cState Maintenance Reimbursement, Property Damage, and Miscellaneous.

Figure 1—Changes in Deflated General Fund Revenues Between 1986/88 and 1994/96

have helped the city maintain stable general fund revenues and are to be lauded, there is still considerable room for improvement in the city's approach to revenue generation.

The main deficiency in the area of revenue generation is the weak link between revenue planning and strategic planning. A main goal of strategic planning is to help a city identify its core sources of competitive advantage and core value commitments. To make revenue-generating activities as successful as possible, they should build on these core competencies and values. In the areas of revenue planning, we have recommendations related to land use and development, updating fee and fine schedules, selling and contracting for city services, and improving the city's ability to raise grant money. In all four areas, we believe that South Gate's ability to improve revenue streams will be enhanced by more clearly linking city activities to strategic priorities and goals.

LAND USE AND DEVELOPMENT

Land use and development is clearly one of the most significant revenue generators for the city. Directly or indirectly, the extent of land use and development accounts for approximately 50 percent of South Gate's overall general fund revenues. In FY 1995–1996, revenues related to land use and development included $4.8 million in sales and use taxes, $1.7 million in franchise taxes, $1.3 million in property taxes, and $1.2 million in business license taxes. The city has a number of tools at its disposal to encourage land use and development. These tools include zoning, active marketing, and the use of financial resources for specific development projects. With the exception of large fluctuations due to proceeds from bonds, loans, or asset sales, the financial resources available to the city's Community Development Department have remained steady at between $5 million and $6 million over the past decade.

The Community Development Department has effectively used these tools to recruit new businesses to South Gate. Chains and franchises such as Miller's Outpost, Burger King, and El Pollo Loco have been brought to South Gate. The department has also been able to attract and retain a number of large manufacturing concerns. Successes in this area include keeping the company Eck Adams from moving to Little Rock, Arkansas; attracting Koos Manufacturing, which generated over 900 jobs for the city; and facilitating the further development of DSL and Care Tex. These successes are particularly notable given a depressed manufacturing economy in Southern California through most of the past decade.

Although the Community Development Department is to be lauded for its proactive efforts in promoting South Gate's economic development, we have two recommendations on how it can more effectively use the resources at its disposals. These include linking development efforts to an overall vision of economic development for the community and using community resources more effectively.

Link Development to an Overall Vision for the City

At present, the city's efforts to recruit new business are not clearly linked to an overall vision for development. Linking business recruitment to the overall vision for the city that emerges from the strategic planning process will help the city build a reputation for having a comparative advantage in supporting certain types of economic activity. A clear and strong reputation can improve the city's overall development effort by encouraging informal marketing of the city. As the city becomes known for doing certain things well, this information will spread informally through exchanges between businesses and business associations both within and outside South Gate.

Use Community Resources More Effectively

A second and related way that the city can improve its efforts to support economic development is to more effectively enlist the support of business and community resources. All the groups that influence land development—developers, real estate agents, business owners, and land owners—need to be included not just in the strategic planning process but also in putting this plan into operation. Through formal and informal contacts with businesses in the Los Angeles area and beyond, individuals in these groups will develop a sense of how different markets are emerging and which businesses are likely to be entertaining expansions or relocations. They should, therefore, be included in the city's efforts to recruit new businesses. We recommend that the city create an informal team of city employees and business and community representatives to create strategies for soliciting new businesses.

UPDATING FEE AND FINE SCHEDULES

A second important area for improved revenue generation is in the use of fees and fines charged for city services. The city provides services to people who live, work, shop, and play in South Gate. These services include infrastructure maintenance and upgrades, inspections, licensing, housing assistance, police protection, and recreation. The city can cover the costs of providing these service through charging user fees or the city can choose to partially or fully subsidize the service by allocating general fund money to cover staff time and the cost of equipment. At present, the City of South Gate does not have a well-established mechanism to ensure that the costs of city services are accurately determined and that the City Council regularly review these costs in determining fees and fines. In 1990, the city contracted with David M. Griffith and Associates for a new user fee study, and the same year the City Council established the South Gate Fee Resolution (Municipal Code Title 2, Chapter 2.76). Since that time, there has been no general review of costs and fees.

The failure to regularly determine the costs of services leaves city officials open to political pressure for unrealistic demands for more and cheaper services even in the face of decreasing revenues and increasing costs. Without a clear understanding of the level of subsidization of existing services, the city will be under pressure to maintain and/or increase subsidies. Although subsidizing a service does distort the market for that service by artificially increasing demand, the City Council may have reasons for choosing to provide a subsidy. This choice, however, should be an informed one. Legally, a city is prohibited from increasing fees in excess of actual costs.[2] However, the calculation of fees can and, according to some recent voter approved initiatives,[3] should include all of the costs associated with

---

[2]A discussion of the legal issues surrounding the determination of fees and fines can be found in Appendix E.

[3]In approving Proposition 4, and its amendment Proposition 111, the citizens of California did not prohibit general fund subsidies to municipal services but did endorse the principle that the costs of services should be known and any subsidies granted

producing a service. These costs include not only direct and indirect costs, but also "debt service, depreciation, capital improvement, replacement, contingency, retained earnings account, reasonable reserve, and other funding requirements associated with the provision of services."[4]

South Gate has adopted fee increases sporadically, with many departments recommending fee increases very irregularly. Broad-scale fee increases have typically been prompted by studies and reports generated by external consultants. Following the 1990 contract with David M. Griffith, fee collections in the form of "charges for services" rose in FY 1991 by 86 percent over the previous year, from $1.791 million to $3.334 million.[5] Since that time, charges for services have dropped an average of 8.5 percent per year through FY 1995, from $3.334 million to $2.327 million.[6] Although the loss of revenue from the PERS Credit accounts for a substantial portion of this drop (approximately $600,000), fees charged for services have dropped almost across the board since 1991. Only fees charged for vehicle impoundment have registered dramatic increases. Similarly, revenues collected for licenses and permits have declined or stayed stable in all but one category. Only animal licensing fees have experienced a significant increase.

To make sure that the fee increases keep pace with costs and to keep track of the level of subsidization, the city needs to review annually all fees and fines. There are two important considerations in implementing this recommendation. The first and easier consideration is technical. To implement an annual review of fees and fines, the city needs to calculate the total cost of the service, the unit cost, the fee per unit, and the total revenues derived from the service. It has been some years since the city last underwent a thorough calculation of costs of services, and there are probably few, if any, city employees who remember the process in detail. To conduct an overall cost

---

should be explicit. Proposition 4 also implicitly supports a principle that users who can afford to pay for government services should indeed pay for them, at full cost and without subsidy.

[4]Ernst and Young (1991, p. 16).

[5]City of South Gate (1994–95, p. 97).

[6]These figures are reported in nominal dollars, thus understating the actual extent of the decrease.

evaluation, the city, therefore, will need to employ a consultant. The contract with the consultant should be structured in such a way that on-the-job training will be provided to key city employees at the same time that the cost evaluation is being completed. This will allow the city to avoid having to hire a consultant to conduct future annual cost surveys. The second consideration in updating fees and fines is political. Decisions about which services should be subsidized and which services should be fully covered by user fees need to be clearly linked to value commitments as determined during the strategic planning process. Without a clear link to the city's core values, choices about fees and fines will appear arbitrary and may appear to be politically motivated.

With a clear sense of costs and revenues and community values, the city's departments will be in a position to prepare comparative schedules (including previous years, as appropriate) and a schedule of recommended adjustments to fee levels. The City Manager should then consolidate these recommendations into a single proposal for presentation to the City Council. The City Council will have the responsibility of deciding which fees, if any, will be raised to recover the full costs of services and which services will be subsidized and to what extent. The City Council should do this by amending the fee resolution. This cycle should be completed each year, just before the beginning of the budget-planning cycle, so that city leaders will have a new fee resolution when preparing the budget proposal for the following year.

SELLING AND CONTRACTING FOR CITY SERVICES

A third avenue to be explored for improving planning of revenue streams is in the area of selling and contracting for city services. Our research and previous studies indicated that there is a healthy market within and around South Gate for city services.[7] Typical services bought and sold by municipalities include traffic signal maintenance, street sweeping, sewer cleaning, parks and recreation maintenance, jail services, ambulance services, and solid waste removal. South Gate has made only minimal efforts to either buy or sell city

---

[7]See Appendix F and The Warner Group (1994).

services in this market. The city has contracted for landscaping, tree trimming, solid waste removal, and plan checking. The Police Department will soon begin selling jail services to Bell Gardens, and there have been attempts to market planning services and vehicle maintenance.

As part of the effort to improve revenue streams, the City of South Gate needs to be more proactive in selling and contracting for city services. Finding a better fit between the city's core competencies and city service provision will increase revenues and decrease costs. By not selling services that the city can provide at a lower cost or a higher quality than other municipalities, it is losing possible revenues. Similarly, there is the opportunity cost of lost revenues to the city for performing services itself that can more effectively be performed by an outside contractor.

In determining whether a city service is a good candidate to be sold or contracted, departments, division heads, and employees need to go through the following decisionmaking process:

- Determine the cost and quality of city-provided services;

- Determine the market price and quality of other providers' service provision; and

- Compare the cost and quality of both.

A first step in exploring the selling and contracting of services is to accurately determine the service's cost. A full cost accounting should include all direct and indirect costs—including personnel, procurement, and accounting services; depreciation costs of any equipment used; and travel time. In considering selling city services, a key issue is determining if the city has excess capacity in either physical or labor resources. In areas where the city has excess capacity, selling services will improve overall use of the city's resources. Where there is no excess capacity, the city will need to buy additional physical or labor inputs and thus may not benefit from selling a service.

Once a team of employees and managers has determined the city's costs of both providing and selling city services, the team should then begin to actively analyze current markets to determine which services are being sold and at what price. This step will include contacting city leaders in other municipalities and actively soliciting requests for services to determine whether the city can sell services at a competitive price. Information should also be gathered on the quality of other providers' services for comparison with the city's own service provision. The third step is to compare the cost and quality of the city's service provision with that of other service providers to determine if there is an opportunity to either buy or sell services.

To demonstrate how this decisionmaking process can be implemented, we worked with managers and employees in the Public Works Department to determine which of their services could be most effectively sold or contracted to other municipalities. We chose Public Works for a more detailed analysis for the following reasons. First, our preliminary research suggested that a majority of the services currently being sold between municipalities are Public Works functions. Second, preliminary discussions between RAND team members and Public Works employees suggested that there was excess physical capacity in this department. Third, the new Maintenance Management System in Public Works provides much of the needed information to determine the cost structure in the department.

We analyzed the market size, typical prices, and cost structures for seven Public Works services: street sweeping, sewer cleaning, graffiti removal, street marking, equipment services, vehicle maintenance, and traffic signal maintenance. Our analysis suggests that street sweeping and sewer cleaning are services that South Gate should consider selling. Traffic signal maintenance is a service South Gate should consider contracting. Graffiti removal, street marking and striping, and equipment maintenance are all markets that are presently underdeveloped. South Gate has excess physical capacity in each area but faces significant barriers to selling these services.

Consider Selling Services

There is a active market for street sweeping. South Gate has excess physical capacity in this area. The city has two sweepers idle in the evenings and should be able to compete both on quality and on price. South Gate also currently has excess physical capacity in sewer cleaning, with the sewer cleaning machine idle 30 percent of the time. Also, there are few competitors in this market.

Consider Contracting Services

There is a competitive market currently for traffic signal maintenance and repair. Santa Fe Springs has aggressively entered the
market. South Gate has high-quality service but because of the cost
of its labor force it has a higher cost structure than other providers.
Given the current market, the city may be able to contract for traffic
signal maintenance at lower cost than the current internally
provided services. Cost savings must be weighed against potential
losses in the amount and quality of service. Liability concerns should
also be considered before contracting for this service.

Underdeveloped Markets

Graffiti removal is not a well-developed market, but it is a market
South Gate could enter through well-orchestrated marketing.
Neighboring cities appear to be spending significant resources on
this service and may be interested in low-cost service provision. The
markets for street striping and marking are not well differentiated
from other street maintenance services. South Gate has excess
physical capacity with its street striping equipment used roughly 50
percent of the year. South Gate's street marking equipment is not
used at all times, although the truck that carries this equipment is
fully used. Since neither market is well developed, it is not clear that
South Gate could earn money by selling these services or save money
by contracting out for them. South Gate has excess capacity in the
vehicle maintenance building, but it has had difficulty entering the
market for equipment services because of the logistical problems of
bringing vehicles to the yard. We found no evidence that this service
could be provided by outside contractors at lower cost.

It should be noted that the city's excess capacity in all the areas discussed above is only with regard to equipment, not manpower.
Selling any Public Works services would require reallocating manpower within the Public Works Department or hiring additional employees. It should also be noted that if the city chooses to more fully
use its capital equipment by selling services, it will need to account
for more rapid depreciation and increased maintenance costs when
setting prices.

IMPROVING THE CITY'S ABILITY TO RAISE GRANT MONEY

As a response to growing needs for resources, schools and other nonprofit organizations (arts foundations, for example) have turned to grant writing as a way of increasing revenue. Particularly innovative organizations are able to raise significant amounts of money this way. Starting a school-based technology program, for example, typically has to be accomplished with funds outside a school's general fund revenues. Schools with sophisticated technology programs typically need to raise several hundred thousand dollars in grant money over a multiyear period. Although grant money can help a public or nonprofit organization supplement its income, raising grant money is not always a straightforward affair. It requires that someone within the organization stay abreast of all relevant grants and awards—someone with the skill and time to craft grant applications—and that the organization have a clear sense of purpose. Unlike general tax revenues or transfers, grants are normally awarded for very specific programs or activities.

Responding to declining general fund revenues, many departments within South Gate have tried to raise money through grant writing. The Police Department, Parks and Recreation, and Public Works have all had some success in raising grant money to support their activities. In pursuing grants, however, these departments are hampered by the current lack of internal expertise in the area. Department and division heads need support in identifying promising areas for grant awards and appropriate grant opportunities and in crafting grant proposals. We recommend that the city contract with a grant coordinator to support departmental efforts to raise grant money. Contract renewal can be made contingent on a successful demonstration that grant writing is a viable way for the city to earn money.

SUMMARY OF RECOMMENDATIONS ON REVENUE STREAMS

- Improve revenue generation from land use by linking development policy more closely to the city's core competencies;

- Enlist the support of business and community groups in putting the city's "vision" for economic development and land use into operation;

- Use the city's goals and values to guide an annual review of fees and fines;

- Support review of fees and fines by making an annual review of costs part of the budget cycle;

- Expand efforts to sell and contract services by more clearly linking city activities to core competencies;

- Consider selling Public Works services where the city has a competitive advantage and contracting for services where it is less cost competitive; and

- Create a grant coordinator position to help city departments identify and pursue grant opportunities that fit well with their core competencies.

Chapter Four

INTERNAL OPERATIONS AND SERVICE DELIVERY

A third part of our overall evaluation was to investigate ways to improve internal city operations and service delivery. The goal of this part of the evaluation was to look for changes to the city's organizational structure and work processes that could yield cost savings and improved customer service. Although we did not conduct a systematic evaluation of service demands and staffing levels, available evidence suggests that South Gate is not overstaffed. With about 37 full-time-equivalent (FTE) employees per 10,000 residents, South Gate is both well below average employment levels for the city governments within the County of Los Angeles[1] and well within the average employment levels for neighboring cities (Table 4). Those neighboring cities with fewer full-time-equivalent employees per 10,000 residents have made more extensive use of contracting in areas requiring heavy manpower commitments, such as policing and water services.[2] Although South Gate's overall staffing levels seem appropriate, the city's internal operations could be improved through a consolidation and reassignment of responsibilities across departments and through a more systematic commitment to business process improvement.

---

[1]For a study conducted in 1994, The Warner Group collected information on 17 full-service cities. They found the median total employment level to be about 80 FTEs per 10,000 residents, with a range from about 45 to 140. These figures do not include employees working for utilities.

[2]Just over 160 of South Gate's employees are in these two areas—135 employees work in the Police Department and 28 work in the Water Division.

Table 4

Comparison of Staffing Levels in South Gate
and in Six Neighboring Communities

City	Population (thousands)[a]	Full-Time-Equivalent Employees[b]	Employees per 10,000 Residents	Adjusted No. of Employees per 10,000 Residents[c]	Service Differentiation
South Gate	92,000	339	38.3	38.3	
Paramount	52,000	225	32.4	43.2	Police contracted
Bell Gardens	42,000	162	46.5	38.6	Water contracted
Lynwood	65,000	214	28.5	32.9	Police contracted; own Fire Department
Maywood	27,000	82	28.3	30.4	Water contracted
Lakewood	79,000	314	31.7	39.8	Police contracted
Norwalk	101,000	360	28.47	35.6	Police contracted; own bus system

SOURCES: Annual budgets, 1995–1996; Census data.
[a]Population estimate for 1994.
[b]Includes all full-time and part-time employees.
[c]Adjusted figures take account of service differentiation; see Appendix G for calculations.

CONSOLIDATING AND REASSIGNING RESPONSIBILITIES

We have five recommendations for changing staff assignments and responsibilities to improve the operations of the city government. They include establishing a Housing Division within the Community Development Department, creating a Public Information Office, creating a cross-functional process improvement team to redesign job processes related to opening a new business, transferring full authority for technology planning to a Common Resource Planning Team, and forming a "contracting" team to consider selling and contracting for city services.

Establishing a Housing Division

The number of divisions in the Community Development Department has been recently reduced by one—through the combination of the Deputy Director for Planning and the Deputy Director for Redevelopment positions into one position: the Assistant Director for Community Development. The benefits of this reorganization are supported by both RAND's and the city's own analysis. Our analysis led us to the conclusion that reducing the number of divisions in the Community Development Department from three to two would reduce overhead costs and improve the focus of the department. This recommendation was included in an earlier draft report. Independent of RAND's research efforts, the city's senior management had also concluded that efficiencies would be increased by reducing the number of divisions in Community Development.

Our research efforts have led us to the conclusion that additional efficiencies could be realized within the Community Development Department by making the second division in the department a Housing Division. Community Development is the natural home for an office that coordinates all the city's programs related to housing. At present, these programs are fragmented both within and across departments. Section 8 and the relatively small Rental Rehabilitation Program, both funded through the U.S. government's Department of Housing and Urban Development, are self-standing divisions within Community Development. The Home Improvement Program, which receives its entire $650,000 of funding from Community Development Block Grants (CDBGs), sits in the Building and Safety Department. The $1.2 million deferred loan programs for first-time low- and moderate-income home buyers is at present run by the Community Redevelopment Division.

Consolidating these housing programs in one division will make it easier for the city government to put into operation the goals set out in the strategic planning process. It may also allow for manpower reallocations or reductions. The present Section 8 division should be turned into a Housing Division that oversees and coordinates all the city's housing programs, with the division head reporting directly to the Community Development Director.

Establishing a Public Information Office

Responsibilities for public outreach and marketing are at present dispersed throughout City Hall. The City Manager's office oversees the Public Access Corporation and City Issues Program and administers a customer satisfaction survey. The city's Public Information Manager, working out of the Community Redevelopment Department, is responsible for the city newsletter; production of marketing videos, press releases, and media relations; publicity; and a variety of other public outreach activities. The City Clerk's office organizes a number of community relations projects and coordinates public access to city records. The Police Department has a number of community-outreach programs directed at recruiting citizen volunteers and disseminating information on police activities.

The division of public outreach responsibility between the various departments creates unnecessary duplication as well as missed opportunities to better streamline information exchanges between the public and City Hall. To plan and coordinate public outreach more effectively, we recommend that the city create a Public Information Office, which would report directly to the City Manager. The responsibilities of the Public Information Office would include

- Coordinating all department-based public outreach efforts;

- Organizing all marketing and publicity for the city;

- Designing and administering citizen surveys;

- Coordinating public access to city records; and

- Marketing services to other cities.

This office should be staffed by the Public Information Manager and Graphics Coordinator currently working in the Community Development Department and by several employees currently working in the City Clerk's Office. Over time, the City Clerk's Office has expanded its activities beyond its basic responsibilities for keeping city documents and keeping minutes on city meetings. The City Clerk's role in the new organizational structure should be refocused on record keeping, including, as will be described below, supporting a shift to a "self-service" delivery model for city records and documents. The City Clerk's Office should have only the minimum number of employees needed to store and disseminate city documents. All employees engaged in public outreach activities should be consolidated into the Public Information Office.

Creating a Cross-Functional Team on Opening New Businesses

Streamlining work processes related to plan approval, construction permitting, and business licensing should be among the city's highest priorities. Efficiently completing these work processes is important not only for providing good customer service to citizens, but also for maintaining South Gate's economic and tax base. The development of a robust retail and manufacturing infrastructure will depend on attracting many new, small business owners. To develop a reputation for being supportive of start-up companies and small business owners, South Gate must maintain a high quality of service delivery in areas related to permitting, licensing, and plan approval. Setting up a new business is a many-staged process involving contacts with multiple departments and individuals. Experienced business owners can navigate their way through the permitting and licensing process with relative ease, but for the first-time business owner it is time-consuming and can be bewildering.

Although South Gate city employees have worked to make it easier to open a new business, our analysis (see below) suggests that more work can be done to streamline work processes in this area. We recommend that the city form a cross-functional team, drawing on employees from all relevant departments and divisions, to address these issues. The immediate goal of the team should be to consider and implement recommendations made in this report related to new business openings. The longer-term goal of the team should be to look for ways to continually improve this work process. We also recommend that the cross-functional team be headed by the Assistant Director of Community Development. This individual has both the necessary expertise to head the team and a demonstrated interest in the area.

Transferring Authority to a Common Resource Planning Team for Information Technology

South Gate's information technology infrastructure has been in desperate need of more systematic planning for some years. The city last took a long-term look at its information technology when it contracted with The Warner Group in 1986 for a Computer Needs Assessment Study. This study resulted in the establishment of a Computer Systems Fund (Fund 93) and a five-year contract for the PRIME system, which currently acts as the city's mainframe hardware infrastructure. Since that time, planning has been sporadic and has not covered all systems. Machines, technologies, and upgrades have been added as current budget funds have been available. Although there are many examples of successful technology systems in South Gate, there are no good examples of systems that use interdepartmental cooperation. Among the most glaring weaknesses is the lack of coordination between departments using geographic information systems. The city now has at least three systems that use geographic information, with no plan for integration.[3]

Under the direction of the Finance Director and the ad hoc committee on Computer Information Systems, South Gate had made great strides in the last year toward achieving systems compatibility across departments within the city. Personal computers have been standardized across divisions, and an architecture has been chosen for a new unified system. Uniform procedures for purchasing hardware and for hiring computer consultants have been introduced. The Computer Information Systems Committee has created a list of new software and systems needs.

The city needs to build on this momentum to create a five-year plan for technology, which will outline priorities and an implementation schedule. The city must also create a permanent institutional capacity for designing and coordinating cross-cutting systems, facilitating the exchange of information and ideas across departments, ensuring that end users are consulted in planning new technology sys-

---

[3]The Public Works Department's Automated Mapping and Facilities Management System (AM/FM), the Planning Department's sharing of Los Angeles County and SELAC data, and the Finance Department's billing system all use geographic data of one kind or another.

tems, and coordinating training efforts. Technology needs will continue to grow over time as departments make increased use of databases, management information systems, and communications programs. Without coordination, departments will work at cross purposes without customer needs explicitly taken into account. A capacity for both long- and short-term planning will help the city reduce duplicate efforts, increase technology compatibility, and foster more effective use of the technology.

To meet these short- and long-term planning needs, RAND considered recommending that South Gate establish an Information Technology Office and an Information Technology Director position. Through consultations with the Finance Director and Public Works Director, we have concluded that a more effective solution to the city's technology planning needs is to make the current ad hoc Committee on Information Technology a permanent Common Resource Planning Team and to empower this team to make all final decisions about information technology in the city. This approach has two advantages over the alternative solution of creating an Information Technology Office. It will not permanently raise the city's operating costs by increasing the number of full-time employees. It will also not force the city to rely on a single individual to understand and be able to service all of the various technology applications presently in operation. Rather, the technology team should be able to contract as needed with technology consultants to cover specialized areas.

To be able to effectively plan and oversee the city's technology infrastructure, the city's technology committee needs to be given an annual operating budget to support its activities. There is, at present, not sufficient expertise within the city to understand the range of technological needs across departments nor the synergies between departments. There is also not a sufficient understanding of how to develop a plan for implementing new technology systems, including planning training for end users. An annual operating budget will allow members of the technology committee to cover their time and expenses as they increase their expertise related to technical systems and issues related to implementation.

Form Contracting Teams to Consider Selling and Contracting for City Services

To allow the city to become more proactive in selling and contracting for services, we recommend that the city form a contracting team composed of both managers and line employees. This team will make recommendations to the City Manager and department heads on services that should be sold or contracted. Members of the contracting team will be responsible for gathering information about the cost, quality, and demand for services in South Gate and other municipalities and to document this information in written reports to the City Manager. To minimize politicization of decisionmaking about selling and contracting for city services, it is important that both managers and employees be represented on the committee. At present, there is a high level of mistrust between management and employees on the issue of contracting.

BUSINESS PROCESS IMPROVEMENT

In addition to changing and reassigning responsibilities, the city's internal operations could also be improved by making a more systematic commitment to business process improvement. Business process improvement is a set of techniques used to enhance overall organizational performance by systematically tracking and modifying the way core work processes are organized.[4] The goal of business process improvement is reduced costs, improved quality, and increased customer satisfaction. The business process improvement methodology is simple and straightforward, involving multiple iterations of three analytical steps. These steps are[5]

- Define a work process by creating a process map;

- Measure process performance; and

- Reorganize and improve the process.

---

[4]Business process improvement can involve techniques such as "reengineering," "total quality management," and "benchmarking." See, for example, Osborne and Gaebler (1992), Hammer and Champy (1993), and Camp (1989).

[5]This summary of business process improvement is based on work currently being conducted by RAND as part of a long-term project with the U.S. Army to improve logistics processes. See Dumond, Eden, and Folkeson (1995).

Business process improvement techniques can be used to improve any work process, but they are particularly valuable for processes that cut across departments and divisions. When a process crosses functional boundaries, employees performing individual tasks may not fully understand how their task fits into overall organizational objectives. Having a cross-functional team work together to map a business process helps employees identify unnecessary steps or waiting time that could be eliminated.

After drawing a process map, the cross-functional team should develop performance measures so that employees can understand the overall performance of the process in terms of time, quality, customer satisfaction, and cost. These performance measures create a baseline against which future improvements can be gauged. Using the information gathered in the first two steps, the cross-functional team can identify improvements in the process design, establish goals that it believes are feasible, and then implement these changes. Repeated performance measurement is needed to monitor the effects of these interventions.

Business process improvement efforts are not unfamiliar to the City of South Gate. Four years ago, the city redesigned its code enforcement operations to improve cooperation between employees in the Police Department and employees in Building and Safety. A team of employees and managers was pulled together from all relevant divisions to share information and do joint troubleshooting. This program has been successful in increasing the effectiveness of code enforcement and breaking down barriers to communication across the two departments. The Department of Public Works has also made a commitment to business process improvement. Public Works has used performance standards and a recently installed Maintenance Management System to track and improve the performance of its key work processes, e.g., street pot hole repairs, tree trimming, water service and installation, and sidewalk repairs. Standards are set through a series of dialogues between a division head, a work foreman, and front-line employees and are revisited on a semi-annual basis. The Maintenance Management System allows employees to track progress in completing tasks, measure the resources required to complete tasks, and benchmark performance against goals.

There are three important reasons for the success of these two efforts. The first is the commitment to systemic rather than piecemeal change. Each effort has involved bringing all relevant employees into a dialogue to solve a common problem. Second, in each case employees have had a clear sense of project goals. In the case of the Public Works Department, there has also been a strong commitment to benchmarking and improving performance. The third reason for success is a commitment to bottom-up rather than top-down change. Although the process has been managed from above, suggestions for change have come largely from employees performing the work.

One important side effect of committing to bottom-up process improvement is the effect employee involvement has on morale. In South Gate, both management and employees believe that employee involvement in the process improvement efforts in Public Works and code enforcement has improved morale. This perception is consistent with a well-established literature in industrial psychology that suggests that the ability to structure one's own work is a very important motivator.[6]

The knowledge and expertise developed during these business process improvement efforts should be harnessed and applied to similar efforts elsewhere in the city government. To support the diffusion of process improvement, we selected two business processes for further research and evaluation: the procurement process and the steps involved in setting up a new business. Both work processes cut across a number of departments or divisions and are central to maintaining a high quality of service to both internal and external customers. Attempts have been made in the past to restructure both business processes. Our analysis suggests, however, that these restructuring efforts have not been systemic in nature nor have they fully embraced a bottom-up approach to change.

Work Processes Related to Setting Up a New Business

Setting up a new business in South Gate is a many-staged process involving contacts with multiple departments and individuals (see

---

[6]The classic work in this literature is Hackman and Oldman (1980).

Figure 2).[7] The Planning Department is responsible for coordinating site plan reviews, which include hearings before the Planning Commission, conducting architectural reviews, and ensuring compliance with zoning ordinances. Building and Safety coordinates construction plan checks with an external contractor and reviews by the Public Works Department and the County Fire and Health Departments. Building and Safety also issues construction permits, then typically conducts several field inspections during construction and issues Certificates of Occupancy. The Business License group checks whether the business owner has the appropriate city, county, and state approvals and permits and issues business licenses. It also checks contractor licenses before construction can proceed.

South Gate city employees have already made efforts to improve coordination between the departments involved in this process (Planning, Public Works, Building and Safety, and Business License), and to provide clear information to customers in the form of brochures, instruction sheets, and flow charts. Our research suggests that the process could be further improved by

- Using a full "case management" approach to planning, permitting, and licensing;

- Developing a shared database for Planning, Building and Safety, Public Works, and Business License; and

- Identifying and collecting data on performance measures (time, quality, and cost).

The cross-functional team on opening a new business, described in the previous section, should take the lead in implementing all three of these recommendations.

A case manager is an employee who serves as a main point of contact with customers, delivering an entire product or service. The business management literature emphasizes case management as a way of simplifying work processes that involve numerous handoffs between functional specialists.[8] Multiple handoffs create the potential for

---

[7]Detailed diagrams of all the work processes related to opening a new business can be found in Appendix H.

[8]See Davenport and Nohria (1994).

RAND*MR804-2*

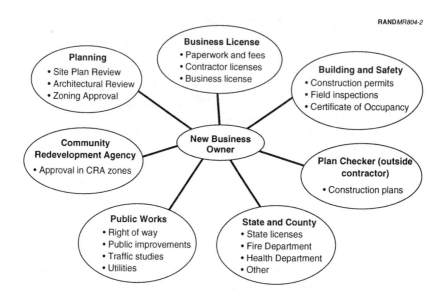

Figure 2—Opening a New Business in South Gate

errors, delays, and misunderstandings within the organization and with customers. The case management approach puts a single individual in charge of the process to act as a customer contact and to monitor the customer's "case" as it moves through the system.

At present, a partial case management approach has been implemented within departments for the business planning, permitting, and licensing process, but it does not fully extend across departments. We recommend that the city move to implement a full case management approach that extends across existing boundaries and covers the entire planning, permitting, and licensing process. For each new business owner, a single employee within City Hall should serve as a focal point of contact. This employee will be responsible for moving the new business owner's application through the completion of all steps in the process of opening a new business and for keeping the customer informed about progress and developments. The home department for the case manager will vary depending on the complexity of the process. For new businesses requiring construction, the case manager should be in Planning or Building and

Safety, whereas Business License employees should act as case managers for new businesses that are not doing construction on their premises. The full details of the case management approach and guidelines for assignment of case managers will need to be determined by the process improvement team.

In addition to adopting a full case management approach, the city also needs an on-line database that ties together parcel-based information from Planning, Building and Safety, and Business License.[9] Currently, paper records are held in different functional areas, making it difficult and time-consuming to respond to customer queries about the status of their projects, e.g., to conduct property owner notifications within a certain radius of a new development. Customer service could be improved and employee time freed up for other tasks if this information were readily accessible on a shared database, with each functional area having responsibility for updating the information related to its own tasks. It would also facilitate the implementation of a case management approach to the planning, permitting, and licensing process, by allowing the case manager on-line access to information about the status of customers' projects whenever they call to make a query.[10]

Finally, performance measures need to be established for the various tasks involved in the process. From the customer's point of view, the total amount of time needed to get through the process is likely to be important. From the city's point of view, completing new business openings with the minimum amount of manpower necessary is an important priority. Appendix G gives a detailed overview of the entire process of establishing a new business. The cross-functional, process improvement team should begin to collect and analyze data on the time and resources required to complete each task in the process, distinguishing between tasks that are performed by city em-

---

[9]Although a system that is integrated with a comprehensive Geographic Information System (GIS) has been suggested, we believe that a relatively simple system that handles the needs of customers attempting to open new businesses in South Gate is a higher priority. The system should, however, be designed so that information can be entered into the more comprehensive GIS that might be implemented later.

[10]An on-line database may also allow new services to be developed, such as on-line information from real estate agents about parcels available for sale or lease in South Gate, or external access by modem for customers to check zoning or project status.

ployees and those that are performed by customers. Measuring both the average and the variability of the time and manpower resources needed can help identify problems that could be corrected. Additional measures could be identified by the process improvement team for quality and customer satisfaction. A shared database can be an important source of data for performance measures, such as total elapsed time of each task, or employee hours spent on a task. Information needed for performance measures should be routinely collected and added to the database so that it can be analyzed easily.

The Procurement Process

Like the process of opening a new business, the procurement process involves many steps and actors (see Figure 3). Purchasing and Accounts Payable, both within the Finance Department, are the beginning and the end of the purchasing process. The purchasing supervisor handles the negotiation of contracts and purchase orders and Accounts Payable issues the checks to pay for orders. There are many steps from the beginning to the end of the purchasing process with possible delays at different stages. The entire process from the issuing of a purchase order to final payment can take over a month. The length of the procurement process is not only burdensome for departments trying to order materials, but it also makes it difficult for the city to negotiate cost reductions from vendors. Our research suggests that the procurement process can be improved in several ways. The first is through more systematic performance measurement. Appendix I gives an overview of the various steps in the procurement process. The Purchasing Supervisor and Finance Director, who are currently working together to improve the procurement process, need to begin collecting data on the time and manpower resources needed for each of the main steps in the process. As with opening a new business, systematic measurement can lead to the identification of barriers to efficient work and to suggestions for improvement.

Although systematic measurement can increase speed and efficiency, performance measurement needs to be supported with the shift to an on-line procurement system. The present paper-based system makes procurement slow and cumbersome. Reliance on paper also creates opportunities for orders to become lost or dupli-

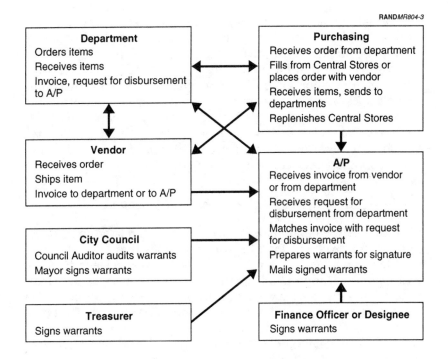

Figure 3—The Procurement Process

cated. An on-line system will allow the departments, Purchasing, and Accounts Payable to check the status of any order at any time, thus allowing them to make timely follow-up when the need is indicated. An on-line system will also allow reconciliations to be done by computer and orders with overaged status to be automatically flagged. Finally, an on-line system will allow ordering from Central Stores to be done more quickly with almost no paper.

A final recommendation related to improving the procurement process is the need to set up a system to pay vendors up front or use partial payment terms when needed to negotiate lower prices. Many goods and materials delivered to the city arrive in partial shipments. Paying vendors for goods as they are received or for all goods before they are received reduces the vendors' costs of doing business. By reducing the vendors' cost of doing business, the city can negotiate lower prices on purchased goods. To effectively implement up-front and partial payments, Purchasing and Accounts Payable will need to work more closely together. Accounts Payable needs to be aware early in the process of the payment terms that Purchasing has negotiated to ensure that payment goes out on time, and Purchasing needs to know when the process is complete. Currently, Accounts Payable does not receive a copy of the purchasing order until the end of the process when the department sends over a copy. Accounts Payable should receive this information at the beginning of the process for all orders, and the purchasing order needs to include information on when payment is due.

Institutionalizing Business Process Improvement

We have analyzed and made recommendations related to business process improvement for two work processes that cut across department and functions. Following Public Works, the Department of Parks and Recreation and Department of Building and Safety have both made first steps toward beginning to measure the time and resource requirements of important work processes. To make it possible for all of these efforts to succeed, the city will need to systematically link its business process improvement efforts to both its technology policy and to its human resource management. As the above discussion makes clear, information technology is at the core of process improvement. Technology is needed to allow for the systematic collection of information related to performance and to link information collected in different departments and offices. Changes to human resource management policies are also needed if business process improvement efforts are to succeed. These efforts require that employees have broader training, better teaming skills, and appropriate incentives. The types of needed human resource innovations will be discussed in more detail below.

FOUR- VERSUS FIVE-DAY STAFFING

South Gate's current staffing pattern is neither helping the city to save on costs nor improving customer service. City Hall is currently staffed on a four-day basis, with a very small staff providing a limited number of administrative services on Fridays. This arrangement is a political compromise between the desire of some city constituents for five-day staffing and the city's interest in maintaining four-day staffing. It has not been clearly linked to an analysis of service demands and needs.

We recommend that the city move to fully implement Monday through Thursday staffing in all employment positions, but consider providing "time-sensitive" services on Fridays. Our interviews with community residents indicate that, for most city services, opening City Hall five days a week would have a negligible effect on customer service.[11] There is a small subset of services, however, which are highly "time sensitive." Business groups, for example, report that not being able to complete a site license inspection on Fridays can cost an owner thousands of dollars. Just as the city would not consider leaving streets unpoliced on weekends, it seems inappropriate to not provide "time-sensitive" services on Fridays. As part of the strategic planning process, the city needs to determine in conjunction with business groups which type of services should be provided on Fridays. These employment positions should be partially staffed on Fridays with the rest of City Hall remaining closed to reduce operating costs.

SUMMARY OF RECOMMENDATIONS ON INTERNAL OPERATIONS AND SERVICE DELIVERY

- Establish a Housing Division within the Community Development Department;

- Create a Public Information Office responsible for overseeing and coordinating all contact with citizens and business in South Gate;

- Shift employees out of the City Clerk's Office to the Public Information Office;

---

[11]Most residents indicate that they can just as easily visit City Hall on Monday through Thursday as on Friday. Other residents who work an 8 to 5 schedule at sites some distance from City Hall would receive lower quality customer service with five-day service. It should be noted that these conclusions are drawn from meetings with a small number of South Gate residents. Without more in-depth surveying of community residents, we cannot be sure that the opinions expressed in these meetings are representative.

- Create a cross-functional process improvement team to redesign job processes related to opening a new business;

- Transfer full authority for technology planning and implementation to the Common Resource Planning Team for information technology;

- Form "contracting" teams of managers and employees to make decisions about selling and contracting for city services;

- Streamline the process of opening a new business by creating a full-case-manager approach to service delivery, an on-line database linking departments and divisions, and clear performance measures for all stages in the process;

- Streamline procurement by creating an on-line procurement database to link departments and divisions and by introducing performance measurements for key steps in the procurement process;

- Set up a process to pay vendors up front or use partial payment terms to allow the city to negotiate lower prices on purchased goods and services;

- Link business process improvement efforts to technology policy and human resource management; and

- Implement Monday through Thursday staffing in all employment positions, but consider providing "time-sensitive" services on Fridays.

Chapter Five

MANAGING COMMON RESOURCES

A fourth and final area of our overall evaluation was an investigation of ways to improve management of common resources. As indicated in the chapter on strategic planning, effectively planning and coordinating the management of information technology, financial resources, human resources, and communication are important elements of achieving high performance. Innovative cities are using cross-functional teams of managers and employees to improve decisionmaking, increase information flows, and support the diffusion of innovative ideas in all of these common resource areas.

Both our own observations and comments made by city staff during interviews suggest that in the City of South Gate operations are heavily department-oriented. At present, mechanisms to coordinate management of the resources that affect all city departments are weak. Mechanisms to support the diffusion of innovative ideas from one department to the next are, similarly, weak. We recommend that the city give Common Resource Planning Teams, described in the chapter on strategic planning, an operational as well as a strategic role. These teams should meet on a regular basis over the course of each year to consider changes and modifications to policies affecting the management of common resources. A first task for each team is to review the recommendations below for each common resource area and to consider how to best incorporate these recommendations into South Gate's operations.

PLANNING FOR TECHNOLOGY

South Gate is in the process of trying to more firmly establish a common technology policy. At this writing, South Gate is in the final stages of completing a request for proposal (RFP) that will replace the existing PRIME mainframe and add much new computing power and connectivity to the city's operations. Along with the new hardware and basic software that will be purchased, there will be an opportunity to revamp some of South Gate's systems. It is our recommendation that the city not move to finalize the RFP until the technology team, in conjunction with the Finance Director, develops a five-year strategic plan for the development of the city's information technology infrastructure. Although a technology needs assessment has been conducted, the findings from this assessment have not yet been formalized into a plan. The RFP represents the most significant investment in South Gate's information infrastructure in close to a decade. It is important that the city use the RFP process to ensure that all its technology needs will be met. Two specific parts of the city's overall technology plan that need to be carefully developed are a plan for implementing the new technology system and a plan for using technology to support business improvement efforts.

Implementing a New Technology System

Research on the implementation of technology systems shows that organizations enjoy the greatest success in implementing new technology when user groups have input into the selection of software systems, believe that software is well suited to their information-handling tasks, and have adequate training.[1] In South Gate's present decisionmaking process, there has been insufficient user consultation and there is not a clear plan for user training. Before the city moves ahead with implementing a new system, both of these issues need to be addressed.

South Gate has learned the pitfalls of not adequately planning for a new technology system. In the 1987 implementation of the PRIME system, potential users either did not feel they had influence over the

---

[1]See Bikson, Gutek, and Mankin (1987) and Richter (1996).

spread of technology or believed that the software was not suited for their information tasks. Many employees never became users of the new system. Some even designed separate methods or systems to accomplish tasks that the PRIME should have been able help them with. Others continued to use more time-consuming non-automated methods for completing their work. Even financial tasks, which were fully implemented in that system, are often done by departments off-line or through custom-designed systems.

Using Technology to Support Business Process Improvement

With the city facing demands for increased efficiency and higher-quality service delivery, using technology to support business process improvement should be among the city's leading technology priorities. As our earlier discussion makes clear, effective use of information technology is a central element of business processes improvement. At present, Public Works is the only department that has fully committed to using technology to restructure and increase the efficiency of its core work processes. The lack of access to appropriate technologies has prevented other departments (e.g., Parks and Recreation, Building and Safety) from following the Public Works Department's lead. As part of the process of creating a technology plan, the technology team needs to draw on the knowledge gained by Public Works employees to outline how technology can be used more broadly within the city to support business process improvement efforts.

IMPROVING FISCAL PRACTICES

To turn from technology to fiscal practices, we have a number of recommendations that would establish stronger internal controls, allow for better coordination of effort and smoother processes, establish a more fully integrated financial system, allow for more complete information to better gauge performance in the city, and provide opportunities to save the city money or generate additional revenues. These recommendations relate to fund transfers, investment policy, risk management, and financial management.

Fund Transfers

The annual budget is a management tool that allows the city to establish priorities and gauges city performance in meeting those priorities. When adopting an annual budget, the City Council grants expenditure authority to each department within major object and account categories for a variety of funds within departments. As part of their normal operations, department heads will need to make transfers within and across funds. Over the course of a fiscal year, there are typically many events and contigencies that cannot be predicted and built into a department's budget from the outset. Although transfers are a normal and necessary part of departmental operations, the City Council needs to have clear oversight on fund transfers. Fund transfers are an important tool to monitor both accountability and performance. The ability of the city to gauge performance depends on its ability to account for whether the goals set in the budget are being met. When goals are not met, the City Council and City Manager need to have a clear understanding of why they were not met.

At present, South Gate does not have formal, written policy guidelines in effect that designate the appropriate authorization level required for common types of budget amendments. The city needs to establish written policy guidelines for the appropriate levels at which authorization is required for the transfer of funds within account categories, between account categories, and between funds. The operating policy in South Gate has generally been that all budget amendments appear before the City Manager and Finance Director and amendments above $20,000 appear before the City Council.

In the process of establishing a written policy, the city should reevaluate current levels of authorization required for budget amendments. The city administration needs to consider where to set levels so that they are low enough to allow for accountability and performance measurement while high enough to avoid overburdening administration and departments. The current level of authorization of $20,000 for some budget amendments to appear before the City Council appears to be high relative to other cities, including cities with larger operating budgets than South Gate. At the same time, other cities generally do not have all budget amendments appearing before the City Manager. The cities that we spoke with generally had all budget amendments appearing before the Finance Director and all transfers of spending authority between major account categories and between funds appearing before the City Council. The transfer of spending authority within major account categories in a fund is generally set at different authorization levels for the City Manager and the City Council. These amendments typically went to the City Manager when they were between $5,000 and $10,000 and to the City Council at levels between $10,000 and $20,000.

Investment Policy

The pressures that cities face for generating revenues have put increased attention on city investment practices as a possible area to increase revenues. At the same time, these pressures are taking place in an environment that places increased emphasis on the need for investment oversight, investment safety, and the protection of public money. The City of South Gate needs a formal city investment policy that includes issues such as the division of investment responsibilities in the city, investment diversification and competitive selection of investments, and goals by which to monitor investment performance. Investment responsibilities, by law, rest with the City Council, which delegates the day-to-day investment activities and overall management of the investment program to others in the city. Currently, investment responsibilities in South Gate are delegated in practice solely to the City Treasurer, which is an elected position.

The city's written investment policy should include information on the objectives of the city in terms of its investments—including safety, liquidity, conformance with legal requirements, diversification, and rate of return. The city is heavily invested in very conservative instruments with the majority of city moneys invested in the Local Agency Investment Fund (a state pool generally called "LAIF"). Investments in LAIF are highly liquid as deposits can be converted to cash within 24 hours without loss of interest. In comparison to other California cities with similar size investment portfolios, South Gate is using a fairly limited range of investment vehicles.

The city should examine whether there are opportunities to earn higher returns through taking advantage of a more diverse investment portfolio while maintaining cash availability and the safety objectives set by the city. As an illustration of the potential benefit of reviewing the city's current investment strategy, an increase in the city's 1994–1995 rate of return by one-half of a percentage point would have resulted in an annual increase in interest payments of roughly $200,000 to all city funds.

Further, South Gate needs a deputy position under the City Treasurer position to provide oversight and expertise in the handling of investments. In most cities that have a deputy position to the City Treasurer, the position is held by the Finance Director to allow for closer coordination between these two offices. It is important that South Gate establish a back-up system to the City Treasurer to make sure that its investment interests are secured before there is any turnover in the elected Treasurer's position.

Risk Management

Risk management responsibilities in South Gate are at present divided between the Administration and Finance Departments. The Finance Department negotiates contracts and Administration handles claims. Administration also handles issues related to worker safety. A recently formed Risk Management Committee, which meets quarterly, works to coordinate risk management activities. Although the present arrangements for overseeing risk management are preferable to those in the past (the City Clerk's Office also used to have risk management responsibilities), further coordination is needed. Closer coordination between contracts and claims may help the city save money in negotiating contracts. Closer coordination would also improve the awareness of the city's management staff about risk management policy. Our interviews suggest that many of the management staff do not know whether the city has a risk management policy and are not knowledgeable about who within the city handles risk management.

One alternative we considered to improve coordination was consolidating all of risk management under one department in the city— either Administration or Finance. Our interviews with employees in each department have led us to conclude that the tasks coming under risk management are varied enough to make consolidation impractical. We recommend that the city improve coordination on risk management by creating a formal role for the recently established risk management committee. The committee needs to become the focal point for setting risk management policy for the city. The committee should continue to include the City Manager, the Assistant City Manager, the Finance Director, and representatives of the safety committee.

Financial Management

Some financial management responsibilities that typically rest in a Finance Department have over time moved elsewhere in South Gate. Housing and community redevelopment have both assumed increased responsibility for managing money, making financial calculations, and processing checks. Consolidating these responsibilities within the Finance Department has a number of advantages. These include ensuring that there are proper checks and balances and internal controls, that there is no duplication of effort, that those with budget and accounting expertise make financial calculations, and that there is consistency in fiscal practices as department director positions turn over. Fully consolidating financial management responsibilities such as bookkeeping, financial calculations, and check processing in the Finance Department may require some reassignment of staff or staff time.

INTRODUCING INNOVATIVE HUMAN RESOURCES MANAGEMENT PRACTICES

A third area for improved common resource management relates to human resource management. Many of the recommendations suggested in this report will require that South Gate have a more broadly skilled and engaged workforce. To successfully work within teams and across departments, employees will need a broader range of both technical and interpersonal skills. To achieve improved service to both internal and external customers and to contribute to business process improvement efforts, city employees will need to become active problem-solvers. To support this transition, the city needs to modify its existing human resource policies and practices. We have recommendations related to performance evaluations, skill development, compensation, and employment security.

Use Performance Evaluations

Effectively using performance evaluations is an integral element of achieving the shift to a high-performing organization. Performance evaluations are an important way for an organization to indicate the types of skills and behaviors it values most highly. In a time of transition, performance evaluations can also be used to reflect how an organization's core values are changing. In addition to signaling organizational values, performance evaluations are also an important tool for individual competency development. By giving employees feedback on how they are performing relative to organizational expectations, performance evaluations can be used to encourage skill development consistent with organizational needs.

At present, South Gate is underutilizing the potential value of performance evaluations. Although performance evaluations are conducted on an annual basis, our observations and interviews with staff suggest that these evaluations are not being conducted systematically and that there is confusion about what performance evaluations are meant to accomplish. We have two recommendations to improve performance evaluations. First, the criteria used for performance evaluations need to reflect the need for a new set of organizational values. Innovative organizations are increasingly introducing explicit behavioral criteria in their annual performance evaluations. The new behavioral criteria, which are very similar for both public- and private-sector organizations,[2] typically focus on evaluating an employee's performance along the following dimensions:

- Technical skill;

- Commitment to work;

- Mentoring and teamwork;

- Customer orientation;

- Problem-solving, analytical skills, and planning;

---

[2]Information on performance evaluations in public-sector organizations is based on our interviews conducted for this project. Information on performance evaluations in private-sector organizations was collected as part of an earlier RAND project. The findings from this project have not yet been formally published.

- Open communication and listening; and

- Respecting the individual and valuing diversity.

South Gate needs to restructure performance evaluations to clearly focus on these competencies and behaviors. The process of re-designing performance evaluations should be coordinated by the Personnel Manager and the Common Resource Planning Team for human resource management. Each department will need to decide on its own the specific criteria to be used in each category.

To improve performance evaluations as a development tool, South Gate should also move toward introducing 360-degree or multipolar performance appraisal. This human resource technique, which is finding increasing favor among both public- and private-sector organizations, uses performance evaluations by peers and subordinates in addition to a review by a superior. Multipolar performance appraisals increase the value and amount of information that an individual receives as part of the performance evaluation process. Multipolar performance appraisals are also a key element of creating a learning organization, teaching employees and managers the importance of feedback and constructive criticism.

Encourage Cross-Departmental Skill Development

Improved customer service, the success of business process improvements, and the ability to implement a case manager approach for new businesses all depend on employees having knowledge of city operations across a number of departments and divisions. Recognizing the importance of building skills across departments, the city has instituted cross-training to improve customer service at the counter shared by Public Works, Housing, Planning, Business License, and Building and Safety. Employees are being trained to handle simple tasks, e.g., garage sale permits and housing applications, for other departments during busy periods.

We recommend that cross-training efforts in the area of customer service be complemented with other types of cross-training efforts. In particular, the city should make increased use of cross-departmental assignments. The goal of cross-departmental assignments is not to make employees experts in all areas, but to make them more effective generalists. We imagine cross-department assignments as lasting several days to a week. Assignments should not be made randomly, but should be tied directly into business improvement efforts and attempts to establish a case manager approach to service delivery. Assigning employees to short stints in other divisions and departments performing related tasks will facilitate both continuous improvement efforts and case management by giving employees a better sense of how their tasks fit into the city's overall operations.

Introduce Performance-Based Pay System

A third way in which the city can more effectively use human resource management is to begin to differentiate pay to reward behaviors and skills that are most highly valued. At present, the city's compensation system is very traditional. It is a job- and seniority-based system, with pay increases linked to upward progression through job grades and job positions within functional career ladders. There are no mechanisms for rewarding individual or group performance[3] and no mechanisms to reward individuals for continuing to build skills and competencies.[4]

The lack of differentiation in the existing compensation system is a problem for two reasons. From management's perspective, promotions are not based on any performance-related criteria. Employees are given promotions within a grade for longevity rather than for adding additional value to the organization. From the employee's perspective, the lack of differentiation diminishes incentives to build additional skills or to take the initiative in improving service delivery. As pointed out in the section on business process improvement, in Chapter Four, much of the motivation for participating in transformation efforts is the intrinsic reward employees feel in having more control over their work. Although intrinsic rewards are important, they will not always be sufficient to sustain employee enthusiasm. True transformation efforts take hard work. It requires that employ-

---

[3]The city has a merit pay system that in theory is meant to reward performance. In practice, however, merit pay increases have become automatic. Our interviews suggest a lack of recognition on the part of employees that merit increases are meant as performance incentives.

[4]At present, the only skill-based pay is a small award made for bilingual ability.

ees build new skills and put in extra hours on the job. Inevitably the question arises, "What's in this for me?"

To encourage employees to continue to develop skills and be proactive, many cities are turning to innovative compensation and classification schemes. Among the most commonly used innovations are broad-banding, gain-sharing, goal-sharing, and competency-based pay (Table 5).[5] We recommend that the city consider selectively introducing a classification scheme based on broad-banding[6] and link progression through pay bands to performance criteria. Broad-banding involves reducing the number of layers of job classifications

Table 5

Innovative Human Resource Management Techniques Used by Cities

Human Resource Innovation	Description of Innovation	Examples of Cities Using Innovation
Broad-banding	Reduced number of bands or levels in a compensation system	Scottsdale, AZ Escondido, CA Charlotte, NC
	Increased pay range within bands	Arlington, VA
Gain-sharing	Monetary rewards given for generating productivity gains and cost savings	Virginia Beach, VA Charlotte, NC
Goal-sharing	Nonmonetary awards given for meeting organizational goals (e.g., decreasing sick days, reducing injuries)	Los Angeles, CA San Marino, CA
Competency- or skill-based pay	Pay based on skill development rather than job classification	Arlington, VA Big Bear Lake, CA
Multipolar performance appraisal (360-degree evaluation)	Performance evaluations based on feedback from peers, subordinates, and superiors	Scottsdale, AZ Arlington, VA

SOURCE: Interviews and city documents.

---

[5]For an overview of performance-based compensation systems in state governments, see U.S. General Accounting Office (1990).

[6]For an overview of the way broad-banding is used in the public sector, see U.S. Office of Personnel Management (1993).

and job grades. Similar jobs across departments and divisions are placed within a small number of classification bands, which encompass a much broader range of pay. By expanding the pay range surrounding each employment position, broad-banding allows employees to continue to increase their salary without having to win a promotion. Employees can stay in the same position but can be rewarded for taking on additional responsibilities or learning additional skills deemed useful by the organization.

As part of a shift toward broad-banding, the city needs to develop clear measures of employee contribution to organizational performance. Developing clear performance measures will allow the city to move away from automatic pay increases within pay grades and reestablish a link between pay increases and performance. Developing useful and equitable performance measures is difficult. The criteria the city intends to use to measure employees' performance need to be decided upon in conjunction with employees and employee representatives to ensure buy-in on the part of these groups.

Our recommendation is that progression through pay bands be linked to a mix of three factors. They are

- The results of a 360-degree evaluation;

- Demonstrated competency-development; and

- Participation on cross-functional teams.

By linking promotions to the results of a 360-degree evaluation rather than to a supervisor's evaluation, the city can ensure a higher level of objectivity while also rewarding employees for exhibiting skills and behaviors that are most valuable to the organization. Promotions can also be linked to developing competencies that the city deems important to maintaining its overall operations. In all cases, rewards given for competency development should be linked to competencies that can be clearly demonstrated on the job as opposed to competencies earned in a class or training session, which are not necessarily related to on-the-job performance. Finally, progression through pay bands should be linked to employees' participation on cross-functional teams. We have made a number of recommendations in the report about the use of teams. Those employees working on teams will be required to put in additional time and effort, with much of this work taking place during nonworking hours. Employees should be recognized for this additional contribution.

Develop a "New" Employment Contract

A final way in which human resource management policies need to be modified is the development of a new employment contract to be developed in conjunction with employees and employee representatives. Several cities we spoke to had made employment security a cornerstone of their transformation efforts.[7] They recognized that employees will not fully commit to business process improvement efforts or needed organizational restructuring if they feel that it threatens their jobs. To facilitate continuous restructuring, the city should make a formal pledge not to lay off any workers as a result of streamlining or process improvement. Internal transfers, voluntary turnover, and early retirements should be used instead as the main means to manage the manpower level. Employees and employee associations for their part need to clearly outline performance-related criteria that can be used to support individual dismissals. The shift toward a new organizational environment will create greater demands on employees' skills and flexibilities. Some employees will not have the will or ability to succeed in this new environment. To support a shift toward high levels of performance, the city needs to be able to remove these employees.

IMPROVING INTERNAL AND EXTERNAL COMMUNICATIONS

The final area for common resource planning pertains to internal and external communications. An effective communications strategy will support the city's attempts to improve both its internal operations and its outreach efforts to constituencies and stakeholders in the community. We have four recommendations in the area of communications. They relate to "self-service" delivery of reports and records, department contacts for new employees, customer survey-

---

[7]These include Vancouver, British Columbia; Grand Prairie, Alberta; Scottsdale, Arizona; and Arlington, Texas.

ing, and developing a common marketing strategy with community stakeholders.

Self-Service Delivery of Documents and Reports

At present, a large number of reports circulate between the departments and the City Council. Also, a large number of documents circulate between Administration and city employees. Our interviews suggest that the City Council, department managers, and employees feel that the present system for sharing information has many drawbacks. Members of the City Council feel overwhelmed by the amount of paper circulating through their offices and do not always have time to read reports when they arrive. Department heads wonder if its worth expending employees' time to produce reports if they are to be added to a pile of unread documents. City employees worry that they are not getting the most up-to-date information on related personnel policies and procedures.

To solve all these problems, we recommend that the city move toward a self-service model for delivery of documents and reports. As with city records that are made available to the public, the City Clerk's Office will become the repository for internal documents and reports. Rather than circulating reports throughout City Hall, a single copy of all reports should be sent to the City Clerk's Office. The City Clerk's Office will also be responsible for keeping an updated record of all documents related to personnel and administration. The City Council, managers, and employees alike can visit the City Clerk's Office at their convenience. Announcements that new reports or documents have been placed in the City Clerk's Office will be posted in the city's main communication vehicles, e.g., the City Manager's weekly report.

Department Contacts for New City Employees

At present, most of the communication between employees across departments takes place through informal networks that have developed over time. Although this works well for employees with many years of experience working in South Gate, new employees do not know who to contact to complete tasks in other departments. To facilitate internal communication, the city is presently creating an internal yellow pages, listing employees by function. We recommend that the city take the additional step of creating a contact person within each department for new employees. This should be an employee with a long employment tenure who understands the operations of his or her department and can direct employees in other departments to internal resources.

Customer Satisfaction Survey

The city initiated a very small-scale customer satisfaction survey at the beginning of 1995. We have a number of recommendations for changes to the existing survey instrument and to the surveying technique (see Appendix J), but we feel that it is important for the city to continue to gather customer feedback on a regular basis. A well-designed survey instrument is a useful mechanism for gathering information on the quality of city services. A satisfaction survey can also be used to gather information on the timeliness of service delivery and variations in customer traffic. Our recommendations include suggestions on content and organization of the survey, on improvements to the existing Spanish translation, and on administering the survey. Oversight for administering the survey and tabulating results should be among the responsibilities of the new Public Information Office.

A Common Marketing Strategy

South Gate has developed a number of tools (e.g., pamphlets, videos) to market the city to business and consumers in other communities. Although the city may want to expand the range of media it uses to market itself, a more pressing problem is to more effectively coordinate marketing efforts with business groups within South Gate. At present, the city is doing very little to work with local business associations or realtors to develop a common strategy for marketing the city. Through formal and informal networks, these groups are well-positioned to get messages about South Gate out to business and consumers in other cities. The strategic planning process should lead to a number of themes and visions for South Gate. These may include a strategy for supporting start-ups and an identification of future growth industries. The city government, led by the Public Information Office, needs to work closely with stakeholders in the community to plan a strategy for effectively communicating these messages to a broader audience.

SUMMARY OF RECOMMENDATIONS ON MANAGING COMMON RESOURCES

- Use Common Resource Planning Teams to plan operational management of information technology, fiscal and budget practices, human resource management, and communications;

- Develop a strategic plan and an implementation plan for the city's information technology infrastructure before finalizing an RFP to technology vendors;

- Develop a cross-departmental plan for using information technology to support business process improvement and performance measurement efforts;

- Develop an explicit policy on fund transfers and consider lowering the present authorization level;

- Develop better oversight of investment responsibilities by making the Finance Director deputy to the City Treasurer on all investment policy;

- Consolidate all financial management responsibilities within the Finance Department;

- Improve coordination of all activities related to risk management by creating a formal role for the risk management committee;

- Redesign performance evaluations and encourage increased cross-department skill formation;

- Create a new performance-based compensation system that integrates both broad-banding and competency-based pay;

- Develop a "new" employment contract, detailing employee responsibilities and conditions for employment security;

- Introduce a self-service delivery system for internal documents and reports and a system of contact persons for new employees in each department to facilitate internal communication; and

- Revise the customer satisfaction survey and create a common marketing strategy with key stakeholders in the community to improve external communications.

Chapter Six

CONCLUSION: AN OVERVIEW OF IMPLEMENTATION

Our evaluation of the City of South Gate's management and organization has led to a large number of recommendations for changes and restructuring. City leaders will be ultimately responsible for making decisions about timing and implementation, but in creating an implementation schedule they should be aware of the logic of organizational change. Research conducted both at RAND and elsewhere suggests that the phasing of the change process is often a critical determinant of success or failure.[1] Successful change efforts typically start with an open-ended communication to build trust and create a common vision for the future. This open-ended phase is followed by a period of negotiation, with actors from different levels of the organization working together to create a blueprint for change. The final phase of the process is institutionalizing new organizational structure and routines by changing incentives and information flows.

PHASE #1: IMPROVING COMMUNICATION AND BUILDING TRUST (MONTHS 1–4)

Organizational change should begin with a process of open-ended communication and dialogue. The goal of this phase of a change process is to build trust and a common vision for the future directions of an organization.[2] This phase of the process is critical to achieving buy-in among all the major stakeholders, without which

---

[1]See Kanter, Stein, and Jick (1992) and Zellman, Heilbrunn, Schmidt, and Builder (1993).

[2]Fombrun (1994).

71

the change process is doomed to failure. According to one recent study, a large number of the reengineering programs attempted by private-sector firms during the 1980s failed because they never earned the trust and commitment of employees.[3] In the public sector, the process of achieving buy-in is complicated by the large number of stakeholders, including not just different employee and management groups within the organization but also by a large number of public constituents.

The key stakeholders in a city include the City Council, City Managers, city employees, business and community groups, and residents. Our meetings and observations in South Gate suggest that the key stakeholders in the city government and community at present do not share a common vision of where the city should be going. Business and community groups do not feel adequately consulted by city staff in planning efforts. Residents feel that many City Council decisions are motivated by politics rather than by a long-term vision about what is best for the city. Employees do not feel included in key decisions being made by City Managers and feel anxious about what management will decide unilaterally. Within the management team itself, there are important divisions about which direction the city should go.

For all these reasons, the city should take seriously the need to open channels of communication and build trust. We recommend that the first phase of the change process last four months and begin with changes that will build team skills, enhance communication, and build trust. The first phase of the change effort should see the beginning of the participatory strategic planning process. Strategic planning at this stage should focus on an open-ended dialogue about possibilities for new developments and departures. It is important in this stage to consider a wide variety of alternatives so as not to narrow in on a limited range of options too early.

Internal to the city, this phase of the change process should see the ad hoc Committee on Information Technology become a permanent Common Resource Planning Team. CRPs should also be formed in the other three common resource areas, and all four teams should

---

[3]Strebel (1996).

begin to share information and ideas about shared problems. This phase of the change effort should also see the formation of "contracting" teams to discuss the city's core competencies, the services it can sell, and the services it should think about contracting. The first few months of the change effort is also the time to work out a "new employment contract" between management and employees, stating the expectation of employees and conditions for employment security. Finally, the beginning of the change effort is the time to lay the foundation for changing performance expectations and performance evaluations by beginning a discussion within and across departments of key behaviors, skills, and values.

PHASE #2: NEGOTIATING CHANGE (MONTHS 5–12)

The second phase of the change process should be focused on collaboratively creating a blueprint for restructuring.[4] This stage in the process should involve many actors within the community and all levels of employees and managers within the city. The goal of this phase of the process is to institutionalize buy-in and to avoid the "not made here" syndrome. There should be no illusion that this phase of the change process will be anything but hard work or that consensus will be easy to reach. No party to either the internal or the external dialogue will get everything they would like, but by virtue of having participated in the planning process all will be more wedded to the final blueprint.

In the external strategic planning process, this second phase of the change effort should focus on working groups and concrete feedback from community members. As the small working groups, composed of diverse constituents within the city, begin to create plans for dealing with specific issue areas, the city government needs to continue to reach out to community members to get their feedback and win their support. Internal to City Hall, this phase of the change process should see the formation of the process improvement teams. This second phase should build on the dialogue within the CRP for technology during the first phase to finalize a strategic plan for the city's technology infrastructure. During this phase of the change ef-

---

[4]See Ramcharamdas (1994) and Hamel and Prahalad (1994).

fort, the city should introduce the departmental reorganizations described in the report in preparation for finalizing the strategic plan. Implementing the recommendations for housing policy will be much easier if a Housing Division has already been created. This phase of the change process should also see the negotiation and implementation of all changes to fiscal policy.

PHASE #3: COMMITTING TO IMPROVEMENT (MONTHS 13–24)

During the last phase of the change effort, two things need to happen. First, the city needs to finalize its new strategic priorities and create internal resource alignment by developing a long-term project schedule and budget for meeting these priorities. Second, this phase of the process should see an institutionalization of a commitment to innovation. We have recommended two main tools that can help institutionalize this commitment. One tool is the customer satisfaction survey. It is during this phase of the change effort—after the city has decided on new strategic directions—that survey of citizen customers should begin in earnest. Surveying should be used to further the city's commitment to continuously improving customer service.

A second tool is the use of innovative human resource management techniques. The transition to a new organization structure will be difficult, and some employees and managers may not be comfortable in the new environment. It is during this phase of the change effort that the city needs to use human resource policies to recruit and train employees with a new skill set as well as to signal and reward the types of behaviors it values most. During this phase of the process, earlier discussion on key values should be made concrete in the form of a new performance evaluation strategy. This phase should also see development of the 360-degree evaluation techniques, the beginning of negotiations on how to differentiate pay, and more systematic thought to the issue of how to recruit and retain individuals who are well-suited to the new organizational environment.

A phased approach to working through the recommendations outlined in our report will ensure that the city is able to implement new organizational and management strategies. Successfully implementing these new strategies will in turn better prepare the city to embrace the more uncertain environment that presently confronts all city governments.

ORGANIZATIONS CONTACTED

ORGANIZATIONS CONTACTED WITHIN SOUTH GATE

Firestone Business Association	Maloney Meat Company
Tweedy Mile Business Association	Ameron
South Gate Chamber of Commerce	UDI Development
DSL Transportation Company	World Oil Company
Southern California Edison	Llovio Ford
Goldy's Chrysler/Plymouth Dealership	Care Tex
South Gate Four Square Church	Shoe Port
South Gate's Citizen Advisory Committee	Rockview Dairy
Real Estate Agents and Developers (12)	Kiwanis Club
South Gate High School	South Gate Middle School

FEDERAL, STATE, AND REGIONAL AGENCIES CONTACTED

California EPA, Department of Toxic Substance Control

California League of Cities

Center for Youth Minority Employment Studies, CSULA

Charo

Contract Cities Association

International City Managers Association

Local Government Commission, Los Angeles

Lorick Associates, Management Consultants

Los Angeles County

National Association of Housing and Redevelopment

Southern California Association of Governments

United States Environmental Protection Agency

OTHER CITIES CONTACTED

Bell, California (Finance, Public Works)

Bell Gardens, California (Finance, Public Works)

Beverly Hills, California (Information Services)

Big Bear Lake, California (Public Works, Personnel)

Carson, California (Finance, Public Works)

Charlotte, North Carolina (Personnel, City Manager)

Compton, California (Finance, Public Works)

Culver City, California (Information Services, Community Development)

Downey, California (Finance Department)

El Monte, California (Finance Department)

Emeryville, California (Redevelopment Agency)

Escondido, California (Personnel, Information Services)

Fontana, California (Public Works)

Grande Prairie, Alberta (Information Services, Public Works)

Lakewood, California (Finance Department)

Los Angeles, California (Sanitation, Public Works, Personnel)

Lynwood, California (Finance, Public Works)

Monrovia, California (Public Works, City Manager)

Norwalk, California (Finance Department)

Paramount, California (City Manager)

Pasadena, California (Finance Department, City Manager)

Santa Monica, California (Finance Department, Information Services)

San Carlos, California (Information Services)

San Marino, California (Personnel)

Scottsdale, Arizona (Public Works, Personnel)

Stockton, California (Redevelopment Agency)

Sunnyvale, California (Information Services)

Tacoma, Washington (Public Works)

Township of Radnor, Pennsylvania (Information Services)

Vancouver, British Columbia (Information Services, City Manager)

Virginia Beach, Virginia (Parks and Recreation, Personnel)

AN OVERVIEW OF SOUTH GATE'S EMPLOYMENT

Our analysis of 1994 Census Employment Data is shown below. It compares employment by industry for South Gate and six neighboring cities: Bell, Bell Gardens, Cudahy, Downey, Lynwood, and Paramount. These cities were selected because of their proximity to South Gate and to Interstate 710. The analysis reveals that South Gate has relative strengths in manufacturing, transportation, and wholesale trade (Table B.1).

Further analysis could give information on what areas within these broad industrial aggregations South Gate may have relative advantages in when it comes to attracting industries. Comparing employment in manufacturing between South Gate and neighboring communities suggests that industries associated with apparel and other textile products, furniture and fixtures, petroleum and coal products, leather and leather products, and primary metal industries find South Gate relatively attractive to do business in (Table B.2).

Further analysis of transportation employment shows that South Gate has higher employment than its neighbors in local and interurban passenger transit and transportation services (Table B.3). Local and interurban passenger transit includes bus service and taxicabs. Transportation services includes travel agencies, tour operators, freight, packing, and inspection. Finally, further analysis of wholesale trade shows that South Gate's employment in this sector is tipped toward nondurable goods. Nondurable goods include paper, apparel, groceries, chemicals, and petroleum (Table B.4).

Table B.1

Number Employed in Various Industries in South Gate,
in Six Neighboring Cities, and in Los Angeles County
(thousands)

Industry	South Gate No.	Percent	6 Neighbors No.	Percent	L.A. County No.	Percent
Agriculture, Forestry, and Fisheries	48	0.2	245	0.2	22,054	0.5
Mining	19	0.1	54	0.1	6,602	0.1
Construction	718	2.9	4,876	4.6	28,656	0.6
Manufacturing, Durable and Nondurable Goods	7,676	31.4	22,537	21.3	773,033	17.4
Transportation	1,728	7.1	4,063	3.8	177,074	4.0
Communication and Other Public Utilities	165	0.7	734	0.7	68,798	1.6
Wholesale Trade	3,006	12.3	9,372	8.9	377,406	8.5
Retail Trade	4,165	17.0	16,780	15.9	764,046	17.2
Finance, Insurance, and Real Estate	665	2.7	5,111	4.8	352,776	7.9
Other Professional, Related Services	904	3.7	9,579	9.1	492,379	11.1
Personal Services	411	1.7	2,051	1.9	85,630	1.9
Business and Repair Services	1,340	5.5	7,247	6.9	383,001	8.6
Entertainment and Recreational Services	136	0.6	2,422	2.3	128,512	2.9
Health Services	763	3.1	7,623	7.2	370,061	8.3
Educational Services	2,001	8.2	7,851	7.4	266,395	6.0
Public Administration	614	2.5	5,031	4.8	135,149	3.0
Undefined	73	0.3	171	0.2	5,903	0.1
Total	24,432		105,747		4,437,475	

SOURCE: Census information provided by SELAC; authors' calculations.

Table B.2

Number Employed in Manufacturing in South Gate and in Six Neighboring Cities
(thousands)

Industrial Code	Southgate No.	Southgate Percent	6 Neighbors No.	6 Neighbors Percent
Food and Kindred Products	274	3.6	822	3.6
Textile Mill Products	75	1.0	76	0.3
Apparel and Other Textile Products	538	7.0	817	3.6
Lumber and Wood Products	188	2.4	344	1.5
Furniture and Fixtures	825	10.7	961	4.3
Paper and Allied Products	334	4.4	792	3.5
Printing and Publishing	314	4.1	547	2.4
Chemicals and Allied Products	366	4.8	815	3.6
Petroleum and Coal Products	452	5.9	268	1.2
Rubber and Misc. Plastics	250	3.3	1052	4.7
Leather	410	5.3	41	0.2
32 Stone, Clay, and Glass Products	0	0.0	614	2.7
Primary Metal Industries	875	11.4	1362	6.0
Fabricated Metal Products	1249	16.3	3694	16.4
Industrial Machinery and Equip.	622	8.1	2717	12.1
Electronic Equip.	681	8.9	861	3.8
Transportation Equip.	87	1.1	6369	28.3
Instruments	62	0.8	86	0.4
Misc.	74	1.0	299	1.3
Total	7676		22537	

SOURCE: Census information provided by SELAC; authors' calculations.

Table B.3

Number Employed in Transportation by Industry
in South Gate and in Six Neighboring Cities
(thousands)

Industrial Code	South Gate		6 Neighbors	
	No.	Percent	No.	Percent
Local and Interurban Passenger Transit	425	24.6	85	2.1
Trucking and Warehousing	775	44.8	2217	54.6
U.S. Postal Service	6	0.3	1396	34.4
Marine Transport	15	0.9	10	0.2
Air Transport	30	1.7	1	0.0
Transport Services	477	27.6	354	8.7
Total	1728		4063	

SOURCE: Census information provided by SELAC; authors' calculations.

Table B.4

Number Employed in Wholesale Trade by Industry
in South Gate and in Six Neighboring Cities
(thousands)

Industrial Code	South Gate		6 Neighbors	
	No.	Percent	No.	Percent
Durable Goods	1422	48.1	5418	57.8
Nondurable goods	1534	51.9	3954	42.2
Total	2956		9372	

SOURCE: Census information provided by SELAC; authors' calculations.

Our analysis gives information on South Gate's past trends and successes in attracting industry. Future growth in South Gate will be influenced by trends in the regional and subregional economy such as the growth of the Long Beach and Los Angeles Harbors and South Gate's designation as a Recycling Market Development Zone by the California Integrated Waste Management Board.

STATE AND FEDERAL INITIATIVES RELATED TO BROWNFIELD SITES

This appendix reports on three recent initiatives related to Brownfield sites by the California state government and the federal government. They are the Voluntary Cleanup Program, the Expedited Remedial Action Program, and the EPA's Brownfield Initiative.

VOLUNTARY CLEANUP PROGRAM

The Voluntary Cleanup Program is run by the California Department of Toxic Substances Control (DTSC). This program works to enhance sustainable development by encouraging partnerships including developers, redevelopment agencies, and other community members to expedite the remediation and reuse of Brownfields. A local example of this program is the "Kite" site in Culver City, which is to be developed into an industrial park. Aspects of the Voluntary Cleanup Program include: (a) a compression of the time needed to investigate and remediate a site, (b) site-specific risk analysis and land-use restrictions, and (c) a reduction of liability claims for those participating in the voluntary agreement.

EXPEDITED REMEDIAL ACTION PROGRAM

The Expedited Remedial Action Program provides incentives for voluntary remediation by addressing key economic issues associated with the remediation and redevelopment of contaminated properties. The bill that created the program (Senate Bill 923, Sen. Calderon, 1994) was supported by both industry and representatives of communities who have become frustrated over slow progress in bringing contaminated sites back into productive use. Attributes of the program include: (a) greater variability in the cleanup standards for individual properties, (b) the inclusion of a covenant relinquishing the state's right to sue new landowners after an initial cleanup is completed, (c) the availability of state funding for orphan sites, i.e., sites where the party responsible for cleanup either cannot be located or is bankrupt, and (d) a streamlined administrative permitting and certification processing.

EPA BROWNFIELD INITIATIVE

This federal initiative provided 50 grants to communities to assist with the process of planning and developing Brownfield sites. Future grants may be available. The grant is being used by Stockton to develop a Comprehensive Environmental Master Plan to assess, remediate, market, and reuse a Brownfield area. Emeryville is using the Brownfield grant to develop a Risk Management Model using California's new policies of containment areas.

REVENUE ANALYSIS TABLES

Table D.1
General Fund Revenues by Source, City of South Gate

	Property Tax	Sales and Use Taxes	Franchise Tax	Business License Tax
1986–1987	866,805	3,963,085	502,595	859,415
1987–1988	946,757	4,760,570	467,056	842,660
1988–1989	1,108,506	5,176,926	470,272	867,857
1989–1990	976,059	5,237,648	501,103	648,239
1990–1991	1,174,118	4,884,950	1,108,702	1,113,814
1991–1992	1,267,484	4,207,296	1,002,968	701,682
1992–1993	1,220,221	4,771,691	1,192,173	862,729
1993–1994	1,179,041	4,667,885	1,195,812	1,223,880
1994–1995	1,256,652	4,660,348	1,200,000	1,000,000
1995–1996	1,325,000	4,750,000	1,385,700	1,200,000

	Other Tax[a]	License and Fees[b]	Parking Fines and Jail Lease	Investments
1986–1987	190,630	509,155	471,670	270,245
1987–1988	290,697	515,993	781,185	561,161
1988–1989	325,948	582,896	618,323	582,440
1989–1990	401,184	756,716	937,599	184,491
1990–1991	432,182	627,622	770,312	400,171
1991–1992	455,005	616,469	482,820	3,661,756
1992–1993	353,640	640,649	405,678	317,771
1993–1994	469,320	617,819	660,495	476,103
1994–1995	556,398	719,317	687,000	367,423
1995–1996	749,000	708,017	684,000	401,523

	Motor Vehicle In-Lieu	From Other Agencies	Parks and Rec.	Internal Reimbursement
1986–1987	2,317,465	1,416,465	313,610	823,685
1987–1988	2,610,975	380,631	387,774	800,974
1988–1989	2,425,539	314,799	365,557	671,117
1989–1990	2,804,736	389,077	425,115	1,205,907
1990–1991	2,953,979	432,340	515,803	1,236,639
1991–1992	3,216,181	26,894	550,242	1,634,457
1992–1993	3,232,174	191,820	503,991	1,284,513
1993–1994	2,942,174	102,416	457,796	1,491,677
1994–1995	2,767,983	109,224	516,000	1,423,380
1995–1996	2,845,000	89,297	525,000	1,465,950

	Police-Related Revenue	Misc.[c]	PERS Credit	Total
1986–1987	137,280	40,390		12,682,495
1987–1988	175,544	16,411		13,538,388
1988–1989	156,131	24,963		13,691,274
1989–1990	252,621	61,169		14,781,664
1990–1991	292,374	53,662		15,996,668
1991–1992	364,778	96,843	1,011,035	19,595,910
1992–1993	321,693	85,258	1,034,000	16,418,001
1993–1994	429,833	446,406		16,360,657
1994–1995	425,177	418,081	223,270	16,330,253
1995–1996	749,000	17,000	432,410	17,326,897

SOURCE: South Gate's annual budgets.

[a]Transient Occupancy Tax, Commercial Refuse Franchise, Real Estate Transfer, Material Recovery Fee.

[b]Building, Electrical, and Other Permits; Plan Check; Animal License ; Zoning fees.

[c]State Maintenance Reimbursement, Property Damage, and Miscellaneous.

Table D.2
Deflated General Fund Revenues by Source, City of South Gate (1987=100)

	Property Tax	Sales and Use Taxes	Franchise Tax	Business License Tax
1986–1987	899,175	4,111,084	521,364	891,509
1987–1988	946,757	4,760,570	467,056	842,660
1988–1989	1,062,805	4,963,496	450,884	832,078
1989–1990	898,765	4,822,880	461,421	596,905
1990–1991	1,037,207	4,315,327	979,419	983,935
1991–1992	1,134,823	3,766,941	897,993	628,241
1992–1993	1,016,004	3,973,098	992,650	718,342
1993–1994	958,570	3,795,028	972,205	995,024
1994–1995	996,552	3,695,756	951,626	793,021
1995–1996	1,019,231	3,653,846	1,065,923	923,077

	Other Tax[a]	License and Fees[b]	Parking Fines and Jail Lease	Investment
1986–1987	197,749	528,169	489,284	280,337
1987–1988	290,697	515,993	781,185	561,161
1988–1989	312,510	558,865	592,831	558,428
1989–1990	369,414	696,792	863,351	169,881
1990–1991	381,786	554,436	680,488	353,508
1991–1992	407,382	551,946	432,286	3,278,499
1992–1993	294,455	533,430	337,784	264,589
1993–1994	381,561	502,292	536,988	387,076
1994–1995	441,236	570,434	544,806	291,374
1995–1996	576,154	44,628	526,154	308,864

	Motor Vehicle In-Lieu	From Other Agencies	Parks and Rec.	Internal Reimbursement
1986–1987	2,404,009	1,469,362	325,322	854,445
1987–1988	2,610,975	380,631	387,774	800,974
1988–1989	2,325,541	301,821	350,486	643,449
1989–1990	2,582,630	358,266	391,450	1,110,412
1990–1991	2,609,522	381,926	455,656	1,092,437
1991–1992	2,879,560	292,680	492,651	1,463,387
1992–1993	2,691,236	159,717	419,643	1,069,536
1993–1994	2,392,011	83,265	372,192	1,212,746
1994–1995	2,195,070	86,617	409,199	1,128,771
1995–1996	2,188,462	68,690	403,846	1,127,654

	Police-Related Revenue	Misc.[c]	PERS Credit	Deflation Value	Deflated Totals
1986–1987	142,407	41,898		0.964	13,156,115
1987–1988	175,544	16,411		1.000	13,538,388
1988–1989	149,694	23,934		1.043	13,126,821
1989–1990	232,616	56,325		1.086	13,611,109
1990–1991	258,281	47,405		1.132	14,369,986
1991–1992	326,599	86,707	905,215	1.117	17,544,910
1992–1993	267,854	70,989	860,949	1.201	13,670,276
1993–1994	349,458	362,932		1.230	13,301,347
1994–1995	337,174	331,547	177,058	1.261	12,950,240
1995–1996	576,154	13,077	332,623	1.300	13,328,382

SOURCE: South Gate's annual budgets.
[a]Transient Occupancy Tax, Commercial Refuse Franchise, Real Estate Transfer, Material Recovery Fee.
[b]Building, Electrical, and Other Permits; Plan Check; Animal License; Zoning fees.
[c]State Maintenance Reimbursement, Property Damage, and Miscellaneous.

LEGAL CONSIDERATIONS IN SETTING FEES AND FINES

Cities are prohibited from increasing fees in excess of actual costs. Section XIIIB of the California Constitution defines any fee revenues in excess of costs reasonably borne in providing the service as taxes. As taxes, these revenues cannot be increased without approval of the electorate. However, the calculation of "costs reasonably borne" can and should include all of the costs associated with producing the service, including not only direct costs but indirect costs such as internal service cost allocations, overhead (general government costs, which may not be charged to federally funded programs, in accordance with OMB Circular A-87), and "debt service, depreciation, capital improvement, replacement, contingency, retained earnings account, reasonable reserve, and other funding requirements associated with the provisions of service, as are deemed necessary and proper by the local government."[1]

OMB Circular A-87 requires an annual cost allocation plan, and for several years the City of South Gate has been contracting with David M. Griffith and Associates to produce it. The plan allocates internal service (and, separately, general overhead) costs to expenditure accounts. This plan may provide the basis for an annual fee and fine update. It may be that the consultants collect activity data for individual services and then aggregate these data by fund. If so, the city need only contract with the consultant to include the raw data in the

---

[1]Ernst and Young (1991, p. 16).

annual plan, and match the cost data with the revenues and units of service provided.

If it is not practical, or is cost-inefficient, to have the consultant provide the cost data by service, then perhaps (at least in some cases) South Gate can account for its costs of services by fund rather than by service. The League of California Cities points out that Code Section 7905 allows cities to aggregate services in calculating costs, provided that those services are "reasonably related." Examples of "reasonably related" services (e.g., public safety: animal licenses, animal shelter fees, weed and lot cleaning, and bicycle licenses)[2] indicate that the services provided under a single fund probably fit well within the range of the definition.

---

[2]Ernst and Young (1991, p. 15).

MARKET INFORMATION ON PUBLIC WORKS SERVICES

This appendix contains detailed information on markets, prices, and costs for the six Public Works services that we analyzed in detail. The six services are street sweeping, sewer cleaning, graffiti removal, street marking and striping, traffic signals, and equipment maintenance.

STREET SWEEPING

There is an active market for street sweeping in which South Gate should be able to compete in both on quality and on price. South Gate has excess physical capacity with two sweepers that are idle in the evenings. Los Angeles County provides street sweeping services. Prices charged by the county are $9.50 to $12.36 per curb mile depending on location for streets and $8.00 per curb mile for bike paths. Table F.1 outlines local consumers of street sweeping services.

SEWER BLOCKAGE REMOVAL AND MAINTENANCE CLEANING

There is an active market for sewer blockage removal. South Gate currently has excess physical capacity in sewer cleaning. The sewer hydro-cleaning machine that is used to remove blockages and perform maintenance cleaning is estimated to be idle 30 percent of the time.

Table F.1

Local Consumers of Street Sweeping Services

City	Cost	Service Provided and Notes
Bell Gardens	$120,000	50 curb miles, once a week 3 times a week for all commercial areas Alleys and painted median, alternate weeks
Lakewood	$341,960	20,800 miles swept last year 200 miles inspected
Norwalk	$280,300	400 miles of streets
Lynwood	$148,000 (not currently con- tracted)	95.5 miles of street Once a week all streets, twice a week for commercial areas City-owned parking lots and alleys, alternate weeks

SOURCE: Interviews with city officials.

If South Gate is successful in entering the market for blockage removal, the city should consider moving into performing sewer maintenance cleaning. Many cities do not do the same maintenance as South Gate and purchase only emergency blockage clearing services. The maintenance cleaning market will be most difficult to enter when cities have a dedicated fee for sewer maintenance because of fewer incentives to hold down costs.

Roto-Rooter is the main provider of emergency blockage services. With a two-hour minimum for each service, Roto-Rooter prices are as follows: regular rate 8:00–7:00, 7 days a week, $205 per hour; after-hour rate, $310 per hour; holidays, $350 per hour.

GRAFFITI REMOVAL

The market for graffiti removal appears to be large but not well developed. Excess physical capacity is limited to South Gate's hydro-blast equipment, which is estimated to be available about 50 percent of the workday. The painting equipment is used during all of the workday. Cities appear to be spending significant resources on this service and may be interested in low-cost service provision. Bell contracts for graffiti removal and protective covering. The removal methods include soda-blast, sand, hydro-blast, and hand scrape.

The contract is for labor and machinery at $65 per hour plus sand and soda.

STREET MARKING AND STRIPING

South Gate has excess physical capacity in marking and striping, but these markets do not appear to be well differentiated from other street maintenance functions such as asphalt repairs. South Gate's striping equipment is used roughly 50 percent of the year. The marking vehicle is used most if not all workdays but the marking equipment on the truck is not fully used. The market for these services is not as well developed as services for street sweeping or traffic signal maintenance. The prices given in Table F.2 are for services provided by Los Angeles County last year.

TRAFFIC SIGNALS

There is a competitive market currently for traffic signal maintenance and repair. Santa Fe Springs has aggressively entered the market. South Gate is able to provide high-quality service. South Gate's well-trained, high-cost workforce will limit its ability to win contracts selected solely on the basis of price. Traffic signal maintenance is heavily labor-intensive. At present, when not working on traffic signals, South Gate's traffic signal maintenance labor force is

Table F.2

Street Marking and Striping

Marking		Striping	
Minimum maintenance order: $400		Minimum maintenance cost:	$900
Minimum new marking:	$600	Minimum new work cost:	$1300
1. Railroad Crossing:	$43.75	From $.10 to $.30 per linear ft	
2. Wait Here:	$16.25		
3. Ped Xing:	$13.50	(the high-end estimate is for double yellow	
4. Slow School:	$27.50	lines)	
5. Stop:	$7.67		
6. Eight foot arrow:	$5.25 each		
7. 12-inch line:	$5.25 per sq. ft		

SOURCE: Interviews with city officials.

currently being used for street lighting and other electrical duties. Selling of this service would require hiring additional traffic signal maintenance personnel or personnel trained in the other electrical duties. Liability concerns also make this a less-attractive market to enter. Maintenance vendors typically must accept liability for lawsuits related to traffic accidents. The risk of lawsuits must be taken into account when pricing services.

There is potential for South Gate to save money by contracting out for traffic maintenance services. Further analysis of the cost to South Gate for its current provision of traffic signal maintenance is needed. The potential for saving money must be balanced against potential losses in quality, the amount of service, and the resultant gains in human capacity.

The rate Los Angeles County used in bids last year was $66 per intersection. Recent bids have been lower. The amount paid for services by cities around South Gate is outlined in Table F.3.

Table F.3

Cost of Services in Other Cities

City	Cost	Service Provided
Bell Gardens	$38,400	General maintenance, 30 signals
		Repairs to 30 signals
Lakewood	$51,000 (contracts portion of total need)	50 intersections (safety lights and street-name signs)
Paramount	$67,950	31 intersections (may include electricity)
Norwalk	$735,400 (not contracted)	80 signals and street lights
		296 safety lighting fixtures (includes electricity)
Cerritos	$43.20 monthly mainte- nance, $25 for flashers	46 intersections (recently received bids)
	$42.49 monthly mainte- nance, $30 for flashers	
	$54.00 monthly mainte- nance, $27 for flashers	

SOURCE: Interviews with city officials.

CALCULATION OF NUMBER OF EMPLOYEES PER RESIDENT IN SOUTH GATE AND IN SIX NEIGHBORING COMMUNITIES

This appendix outlines how we calculated the number of employees per resident in South Gate and in six neighboring communities. In each city, to reach a figure for full-time-equivalent employees, we added the total number of full-time employees to the number of full-time-equivalent part-time employees. Average number of hours worked by a part-time employee was provided by each city's Personnel or Payroll Departments. Table G.1 shows how we reached a total full-time-equivalent count for each city.

Using this full-time-equivalent figure, we then calculated an adjusted full-time-equivalent figure by taking account of service differentiation in the seven cities.

Table G.1

Estimated Number of Full-Time-Equivalent Employees

City	Full-Time Employees	Part-Time Employees	Avg. Hours Worked per Year	Part-Time Converted to Full-time	Total Full-Time Equivalent
South Gate	339	50	550	13.75	352.75
Paramount	108	121	1000	60.5	168.5
Bell Gardens	136	60	575	17.25	153.25
Lynwood	105	140	1150	80.5	185.5
Maywood	66	22	927	10.2	76.2
Lakewood	179	228	631.5	72	251
Norwalk	200	250	700.0	87.5	287.5

To estimate the additional number of employees needed to provide police services for Lynwood, Lakewood, and Norwalk, we calculated the average expenditure per police employee for the four cities that have their own Police Departments. Paramount contracts for most of its police services, but its budget gives detailed information on expenditures and services received, allowing it to be included in the average expenditure calculation. Using the average expenditure per police employee, we then got information on Lynwood, Lakewood, and Norwalk's expenditures on police services. Using these two numbers, we arrived at an estimate for the three cities. Tables G.2 and G.3 outline these calculations in detail.

To estimate the number of additional water employees for Bell Gardens and Maywood, we calculated the total number of water employees per citizen for the two full-service cities in our sample— South Gate and Lakewood. Of the seven cities, these are the only two

Table G.2

Calculation of Expenditures per Police Employee

City	Police Expenditure ($ thousands)	No. of Police Employees	Expenditure per Employee ($ thousands)
Southgate	12,273.7	135.7	90.4
Bell Gardens	7,410.5	74.5	99.5
Maywood	1,971.4	42.0	47.0
Paramount [a]	6,364.8	78.6[b]	92.8
Average			82.4

[a]City employees plus contract with Sheriff; does not include Sky Knight.

[b]Includes Paramount employees (23) and 111,272 hours purchased, calculated at 2,000 hours per FTE.

Table G.3

Estimate of the Number of Police Employees

City	Police Expenditures ($ thousands)	Police Employees at Avg. Expend
Norwalk	7,966.3	97
Lynwood	5,214.5	63
Lakewood[a]	5,171.2	63

[a]Does not include Sky Knight.

that meet all their own water needs. The average number of water employees per 10,000 residents in these two cities was .22. Using this figure, we estimate nine additional full-time-equivalent water employees for Bell Gardens and six for Maywood.

Finally, we got information from Lynwood about the number of employees in its Fire Department and from Norwalk about the number of employees needed to run its bus system. With all this information, we calculated an adjusted number of employees and adjusted number of employees per 10,000 residents for each of the seven cities. The adjusted number of employees is the sum of total full-time-equivalents plus the estimated number of police employees and estimated number of water employees minus the fire or bus employees. See Table G.4.

Table G.4

Adjustments to Number of Employees

City	Population	Total FTE	Police (+)	Water (+)	Fire or Bus (-)	Adjusted Total	Adjusted Ratio per 10,000
South Gate	92,000	339	n/a	n/a	n/a	353	38.3
Paramount	52,000	169	56	n/a	n/a	225	43.2
Bell Gardens	42,000	153	n/a	9	n/a	162	38.6
Lynwood	65,000	186	63	n/a	35	214	32.9
Maywood	27,000	76	n/a	6	n/a	82	30.4
Lakewood	79,000	251	63	n/a	n/a	314	39.8
Norwalk	101,000	288	97	n/a	25	360	35.6

WORK PROCESSES RELATED TO OPENING A NEW BUSINESS

Figures H.1 to H.3 show the steps involved in establishing a business in South Gate. The process follows one of three paths through the Planning Department (shown in Figure H.1). First, if construction is planned on a site that is larger than 15,000 square feet or if a Conditional Use Permit (CUP) (such as a liquor license) is needed, a Site Plan Review and a hearing before the Planning Commission are required. Second, if construction will be on a site of less than 15,000 square feet and no Conditional Use Permit is needed, an Architectural Review (but no formal hearing) is required. In either of these two cases, after the site plans have been approved, detailed construction plans must be submitted and approved by the Planning Department to ensure that they correspond with the site plan.

The construction plans are then handed off to the Building and Safety Department (see Figure H.2), where they are concurrently reviewed by the city Public Works Department, and the county Fire and Health Departments; then they are sent to an external plan checker. When these plans have been approved, Business License checks whether the contractor has the appropriate city and state licenses and insurance, and Building and Safety issues construction permits. Several field inspections are normally needed during construction work, ending with a final inspection.

The third path in Figure H.1 is the simplest. If the new business needs no construction or Conditional Use Permit, the Planning Department only needs to check whether it complies with zoning ordinances, and the business owner does not need to complete the steps in Figure H.2. Finally, all three types of businesses must obtain a business license and a certificate of occupancy, as shown in Figure H.3.

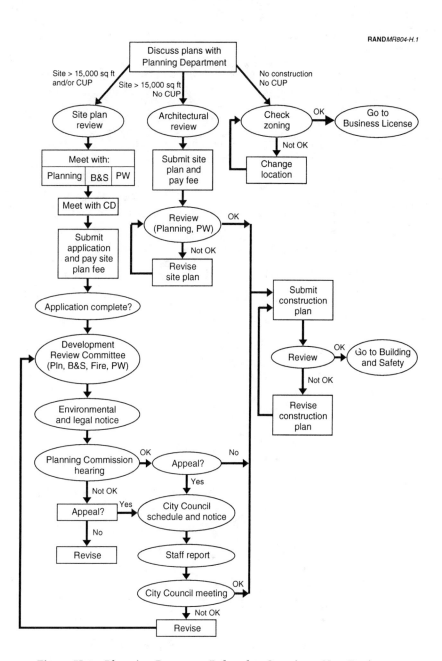

RANDMR804-H.1

Figure H.1—Planning Processes Related to Opening a New Business

RAND*MR804-H.2*

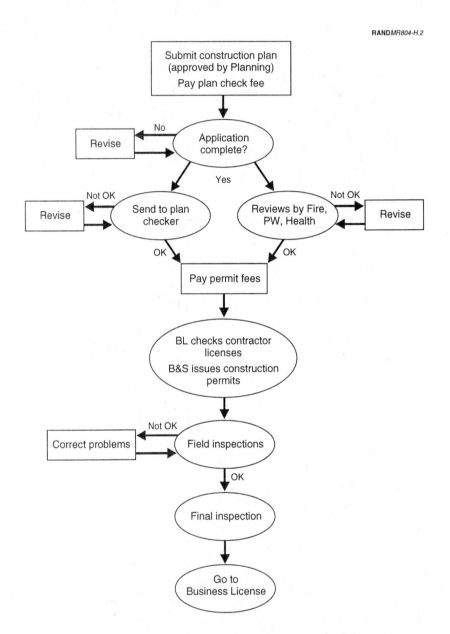

**Figure H.2—Building and Safety Processes Related to
Opening a New Business**

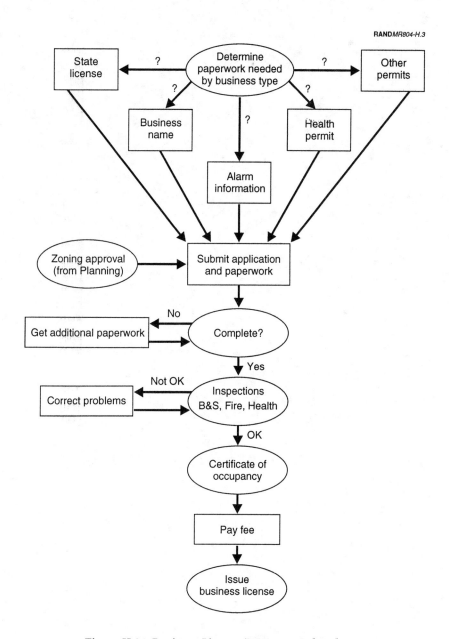

**Figure H.3—Business License Processes Related to
Opening a New Business**

OVERVIEW OF THE PURCHASING PROCESS

ITEMS FROM CENTRAL STORES

Figure I.1 shows the procedure for ordering items from the city's Central Stores. If the item is listed in the Central Stores Catalog as being in stock, the department will order the item on a stores order form. If the item is in stock in sufficient numbers, Central Stores will deliver it and obtain a receipt. Note that this process depends on the accuracy of the Central Stores Catalog, which is updated only about three times per year. Delay occurs when the catalog is incorrect, requiring Central Stores to confer with the customer department. Additionally, the stores' order form can be lost between the customer department and Central Stores, or the customer department may fail to receive or record Central Stores' notification of unavailability. In either case, the customer believes that the item is on its way, while Central Stores either has no knowledge of the order or is awaiting instructions.

PURCHASE ORDERS

Figure I.2 shows the process for using a purchase order or ordering directly from the vendor. Note that the vendor may send the material either to the ordering department or to the Purchasing Department. If the vendor sends the material to Purchasing, then Purchasing has to deliver it to the customer department, creating an extra step in the process. If the vendor sends the item directly to the ordering department, then Purchasing has no way of clearing its purchase order except by making reconciliations with either the department or with Accounts Payable (A/P). These reconciliations are tedious, but until the records are reconciled there is uncertainty within the system of the status of the order.

Note also that the vendor may send the invoice either to the ordering department or directly to A/P. If the vendor sends the invoice to A/P, then A/P has to send it back to the department so the department can assemble the documentation in the Request for Disbursement. Alternatively (not noted in the process chart), A/P may notify the department to prepare the Request for Disbursement, or it may receive the documentation from the department and prepare the Request for Disbursement itself. In any case, several unnecessary steps are involved.

The delays involved in waiting for a council meeting for the council to approve payment has been treated in another section of this report.

RAND*MR804-I.1*

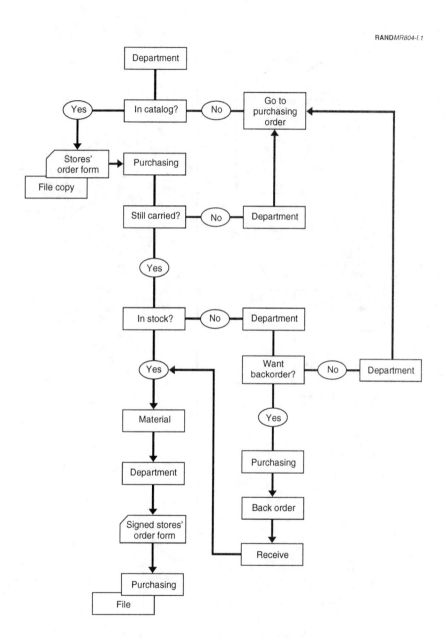

Figure I.1—Ordering from Central Stores

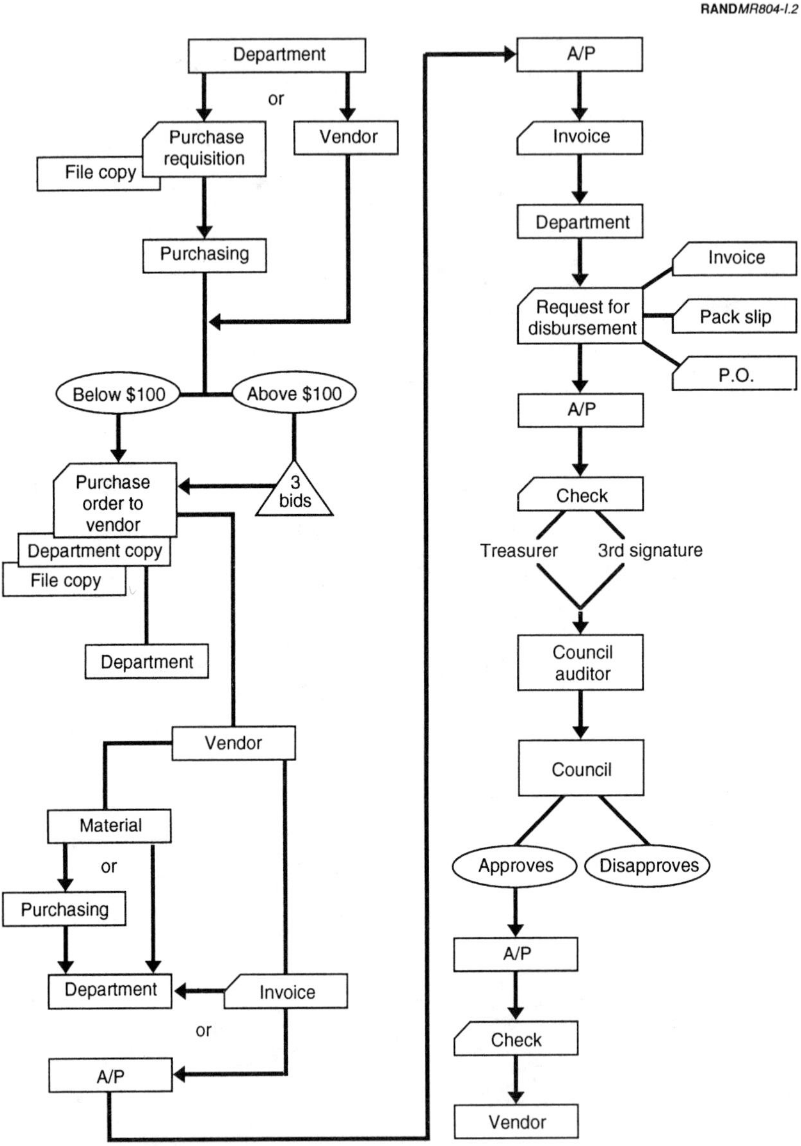

Figure I.2—Ordering from a Vendor

IMPROVING THE CUSTOMER SATISFACTION SURVEY

As part of our evaluation, RAND's Survey Research Group (SRG) was asked to review and make recommendations for improving South Gate's customer satisfaction survey. The SRG was established in 1972 to provide RAND with an in-house capability for conducting primary data collection. SRG is made up of policy analysts and survey methodologists specializing in the technical aspects of survey research. The SRG has a number of recommendations for improving both the existing survey instrument and surveying techniques. These recommendations have been built into a sample survey form, which can be found in Appendix K. The form has also been translated into Spanish (see Appendix L).

ADDITION OF DEMOGRAPHIC ITEMS

SRG suggests several content additions. First, we have added and strategically placed commonly used demographic items (i.e., age, gender, race) that will provide data on who is completing the survey, who City of South Gate customers are, and where they live (i.e., their zip codes). The previous version of the survey gave respondents the option of supplying their name, address, and telephone number. Although useful in deriving a sample of citizens with which one could conduct future surveys, we did not feel such information alone adequately described respondents. Because of the importance of demographic items, it is advisable to make the most important demographic items "required" items. A higher rate of refusal can be expected for demographic items; therefore, we have placed these "required" items at the end of the survey immediately followed by the request for name and address. Respondents are more likely to complete these items if they have had an opportunity to give their opinions first.

SURVEY INSTRUCTIONS

We recommend that instructions for completing the survey be specific and, as much as possible, not be subject to individual interpretation. We begin by appealing to the citizen as an individual (i.e., "Dear Citizen of South Gate"). This is very important in that it attempts to instill a sense of responsibility in the respondent. "Suggested language" for the previous survey asked respondents to "think about the service you have received either today or in the past." Because City Hall employees and procedures have probably changed over time, we strongly recommend that respondents be asked to complete their surveys based on their most up-to-date experiences. We also suggest that respondents complete their surveys after they have completed their business for the day. The proposed instructions are theoretically designed to have all respondents complete their surveys at comparable times and for comparable visits. We have placed these instructions on the survey itself, further standardizing procedures.

ORDERING OF ITEMS AND OTHER CONTENT CHANGES

As reported by Donald Garry in an internal South Gate document, citizens responding to the previous survey appeared to be confused by the form, checking off only one category for the first item when what was desired was a rating for each item. We feel the survey should begin with the identification of a department. Because we feel it is possible some respondents may have visited more than one department on the day they complete the survey, we propose asking respondents to choose the department they spent the most time at. We have included an "Other" department response but do not know if it is applicable.

Because we feel it is probable that citizens may have been assisted by more than one City Hall employee on a given day, we suggest asking respondents how many employees have helped them on a given day. We then recommend instructing respondents to answer the next set of questions "in reference to the department they spent the most time with." We have elaborated on the previous survey's request for a rating on "courtesy, helpfulness, ability to answer questions and overall satisfaction with service" with the intention of making it clearer to the respondent whom they should be rating. Instead of using the previous survey's four-point scale, we propose using a more widely used and tested five-point satisfaction scale. We feel this scale is superior in that it includes a neutral response option and that it specifically asks respondents to rate in terms of their satisfaction. We have also added a question asking about customer time spent waiting because it is widely used on customer service surveys. We propose that further data on customer time spent at City Hall be collected by requesting the start and end times of the respondent's visit. Date and time of visit should be useful in identifying busy periods of the month and week.

Achieving a high rate of response to most surveys depends on a respondent's perceived anonymity. It is very important that the respondent understand that responses will not adversely affect the services he or she receives at City Hall. The previous survey asked respondents to return their completed form to "the counter." This may explain the seemingly positively skewed responses to the previous survey. SRG suggests, for this reason, that respondents drop their surveys into boxes conveniently stationed at all exits to City Hall. These boxes should appear secure and official and should read "Customer Survey Return" in both English and Spanish.

SPANISH TRANSLATION

Our Spanish-language translation specialist reviewed the Spanish version of the previous survey and found that the placement of the Spanish version department categories do not correspond to the English version placement. In addition, several key phrases and words were translated incorrectly. For example, the previous version of the survey used "pobre" for the English equivalent "poor." In Spanish, "pobre" is more commonly used when referring to a lack of material possessions. We have provided a translation of the proposed survey (see Appendix L) that has been examined by two experienced translators who are in agreement on the final translation.

ADMINISTRATION OF THE SURVEY

City Hall employees should be instructed to distribute surveys to all customers visiting their counter. The survey results will be the most valuable if this practice is strictly followed. With this method, there is always the danger of employees distributing surveys to only those customers whom they think will give them and City Hall a favorable review. A few suggestions for overcoming this potential bias are: tracking the number of counter transactions and the number of surveys handed out using number labeled surveys; intermittent monitoring of survey administration procedures; trusting City Hall employees.

We recommend distributing surveys to 100 percent of the customers visiting City Hall counters until at least 200 completed surveys have been received from each selected department. If this number is too large for available staff to manage, lower completion goals could be set for departments with lower customer volume. However, it is important to get equal numbers of completed surveys for each department to be able to make useful comparisons. We suggest that the survey be administered twice annually, taking into consideration fluctuations in customer volume during different periods of each month.

REVISED ENGLISH SURVEY

CITY OF SOUTH GATE CUSTOMER SURVEY
"HOW ARE WE DOING?"

Dear Citizen of South Gate,

In order to help us better serve you, please take a few moments to evaluate the services you received today at City Hall. Please do this after you have completed the business you are here for today.

Which department served you today? (If more than one department, choose the department you spent the most time at.)

(Check One Box)
- ❑ Administration/Personnel
- ❑ Business License
- ❑ Community Development
- ❑ Housing
- ❑ Other Department
  Specify: _____

- ❑ Building & Safety
- ❑ City Clerk's Office
- ❑ Finance/Water Bill Payments
- ❑ Public Works

How many employees in this department did you talk with today? _____

How much time did you spend waiting while completing business with this department today? (Estimate total time spent waiting.) _____

Referring to the employees who helped you, please tell us how satisfied you were with the following:

(Circle One Number On Each Line)	Very Satisfied	Moderately Satisfied	Neither Satisfied Nor Dissatisfied	Moderately Dissatisfied	Very Dissatisfied
a. The personal manner (courtesy, respect, friendliness) of the employees?	1	2	3	4	5
b. The helpfulness of the employees?	1	2	3	4	5
c. The employees' ability to answer your questions?	1	2	3	4	5
d. Overall, how satisfied are you with today's visit to city hall?	1	2	3	4	5

Date: _____   Your home zip code: _____   Your age: _____   ❑ Male ❑ Female

Are you:

(Check One Box)
- ❑ Asian/Pacific Islander
- ❑ Black/African American
- ❑ White/Caucasian

- ❑ Hispanic/Latino
- ❑ Other Race
  Specify: _____

COMMENTS/RECOMMENDATIONS TO IMPROVE OUR SERVICES

_____

_____

OPTIONAL   Name _____   Telephone ( ) _____

Address _____
         Street Number   City

THANK YOU!! PLEASE DROP THIS SURVEY INTO ONE OF THE BLUE BOXES SET UP AT ALL EXITS. BOXES ARE MARKED "CUSTOMER SURVEY RETURN".

REVISED SPANISH SURVEY

CIUDAD DE SOUTH GATE ENCUESTA AL CONSUMIDOR
"¿QUE TAL LO ESTAMOS HACIENDO?"

Estimado residente de la Ciudad de South Gate,

Para mejor servirle, por favor tome un momento para comentar sobre los servicios que recibió hoy en su visita a este Ayuntamiento. Por favor, complete esta encuesta después de terminar con todos los asuntos que vino a arreglar aquí.

¿Qué departamento le atendió a usted hoy? (Si le atendieron más de uno, elija el departamento donde pasó más tiempo.)

(Elija Uno)
- ❏ Administración/Personal (Relaciones Humanas)
- ❏ Licencias para Empresas
- ❏ Desarrollo Comunitario
- ❏ Vivienda
- ❏ Otro Departamento
  Especifique: _____

- ❏ Construcción y Seguridad
- ❏ Oficina del Secretario del Ayuntamiento
- ❏ Finanzas/Pagos de Facturas de Agua
- ❏ Obras Públicas

¿Con cuántos empleados de este departamento habló usted hoy? _____

¿Cuánto tiempo tuvo que esperar para arreglar sus asuntos en este departamento hoy?

(Piense en el tiempo total que tuvo que esperar.) _____

Acuérdese de los empleados que le atendieron hoy, y por favor díganos que tan satisfecho se sintió con lo siguiente:

(Elija Uno En Cada Linea)	Muy Satisfecho	Algo Satisfecho	Ni Satisfecho Ni Insatisfecho	Algo Insatisfecho	Muy Insatisfecho
a. ¿El trato personal (la cortesía, respeto y amabilidad) de los empleados que le atendieron?	1	2	3	4	5
b. ¿La disponibilidad para ayudarle de los empleados que le atendieron?	1	2	3	4	5
c. ¿La capacidad de los empleados que le atendieron para contestar sus preguntas?	1	2	3	4	5
d. Al considerar todo, ¿qué tan satisfecho se sintió con su visita al Ayuntamiento hoy?	1	2	3	4	5

Fecha: _____ Código postal de su domicilio: _____ Su edad: _____ ❏ Hombre ❏ Mujer

¿Es usted?:

(Elija Uno)
- ❏ Asiático/Originario de las Islas Pacíficas
- ❏ Negro/Afro-americano
- ❏ Blanco/Anglo

- ❏ Hispano/Latino
- ❏ De otra raza
  Especifique: _____

COMENTARIOS O RECOMENDACIONES PARA MEJORAR NUESTRO SERVICIO

_____

_____

OPCIONAL Nombre _____ Teléfono (.) _____

Dirección _____
   Número y calle   Ciudad

MUCHAS GRACIAS!! POR FAVOR PONGA ESTA ENCUESTA EN UNO DE LOS BUZONES AZULES QUE SE ENCUENTRAN EN TODAS LAS SALIDAS DEL EDIFICIO. LOS BUZONES TIENEN UN LETRERO QUE DICE "REGRESO DE ENCUESTAS DEL CONSUMIDOR".

BIBLIOGRAPHY

Bartsch, C., and E. Collator, *Coming Clean for Economic Development, A Resource Book on Environmental Cleanup and Development Opportunities*, Northeast-Midwest Institute, 1995.

Bikson, Tora K., and J. D. Eveland, *The Interplay of Work Group Structures and Computer Support*, RAND, N-3429-MF, 1990.

Bikson, Tora K., Barbara A. Gutek, and Don A. Mankin, *Implementing Computerized Procedures in Office Settings: Influences and Outcomes*, RAND Institute for Research on Interactive Systems, R-3077-NSF/IRIS, October 1987

Birch, D., A. Haggerty, and W. Parsons, *Entrepreneurial Hot Spots, The Best Places in America to Start and Grow a Company*, Cognetics, 1994.

Blackerby, Phillip, "Strategic Planning: An Overview for Complying with GPRA," *Armed Forces Comptroller*, Winter 1994.

Blinder, Alan S. (ed.), *Paying for Productivity: A Look at the Evidence*, The Brookings Institution, Washington, D.C., 1990.

Brownfields Forum, *Recycling Land for Chicago's Future*, Final Report and Action Plan, prepared by the Department of Planning and Development, City of Chicago, November 1995.

California Municipal Revenue Sources Handbook, League of California Cities, Sacramento, California, 1995.

Camp, Robert, *Benchmarking: The Search for Industry Best Practices That Lead to Superior Performance*, ASQC Quality Press, Milwaukee, Wisconsin, 1989.

City of Bell Gardens, 1995–1996 Budget.

City of Lakewood, Two Year Adopted Budget 1994–1996.

City of Lynwood, Annual Budget FY 1995–1996, *A City Meeting Challenges.*

City of Maywood, Annual Budget, 1995–1996 Fiscal Year.

City of Norwalk, Adopted Budget, Fiscal Year 1996.

City of Paramount, 1996 Budget.

City of South Gate, Adopted Budget FY 1995–1996, 1994–1995, 1993–1994, 1992–1993, 1991–1992, 1990–1991, 1989–1990.

City of South Gate, *Comprehensive Annual Financial Report, Fiscal Year 1994–95.*

Culver City Redevelopment Agency, Annual Budget 1995–1996.

Davenport, Thomas, *Process Innovation: Reengineering Work Through Information Technology*, Harvard Business School Press, Boston, Massachusetts, 1993.

Davenport, Thomas, and Nitia Nohria, "Case Management and the Integration of Labor," *Sloan Management Review*, Winter 1994.

Dumond John, Rick Eden, and John Folkeson, *Velocity Management: An Approach for Improving the Responsiveness and Efficiency of Army Logistics Processes*, RAND, DB-126-1-A, 1995.

Ernst and Young, *Article XIIIB Appropriations Limit: Uniform Guidelines*, League of California Cities, Sacramento, California, March 1991.

Fombrun, Charles, *Leading Corporate Change*, McGraw-Hill Inc., New York, N.Y., 1994.

Gore, Al, *From Red Tape to Results: Creating a Government That Works Better and Costs Less*, Office of the Vice President, Washington, D.C., 1993.

Hackman, J. Richard, and Greg Oldman, *Work Redesign*, Addison-Wesley Publishing Company, Reading, Massachusetts, 1980.

Hamel, G., and C. K. Prahalad, *Competing for the Future*, Harvard Business School Press, Boston, Massachusetts, 1994.

Hammer, Michael, and James Champy, *Reengineering the Corporation*, HarperCollins Publishers, Inc., New York, 1993.

Hernandez, Shawn, "Information Technology Vision," City of Sunnyvale, Memo to the Executive Committee, Sunnyvale, California, May 10, 1994.

Kanter, Rosabeth Moss, Barry A. Stein, and Todd D. Jick, *The Challenge of Organizational Change: How Companies Experience It and Leaders Guide It*, Free Press, New York, 1992.

Katzenback, John R., and Douglas K. Smith, *The Wisdom of Teams*, Harvard Business School Press, Boston, Massachusetts, 1993.

Koyasako, S. K., "Brownfields, California's EPA's Policy and Legal Response," *Land Use & Environmental Forum*, Summer 1995.

Larson T., and L. Finney, *Rebuilding South Central Los Angeles: Myths, Realities, and Opportunities*, California State University, Los Angeles, California, 1996.

League of California Cities, *California Municipal Revenue Sources Handbook*, League of California Cities, Sacramento, California, 1995.

Lewis Leslie, James A. Coggin, and C. Robert Roll, *The United States Special Operations Common Resource Management Process: An Application of the Strategy-to-Tasks Framework*, RAND, MR-445-A/SOCOM, 1994.

Local Government Commission, *Participation Tools for Better Land-Use Planning*, The Center for Livable Communities Project, Sacramento, California, May 1995.

Management Services Institute, *Fees and Finances of the City of South Gate, California,* La Mirada, California, April 1983.

Menchik, Mark David, Judith Fernandez, and Michael Caggiano, *How Fiscal Restraint Affects Spending and Services in Cities,* RAND, R-2644-FF/RC, January 1982.

Mintzberg, Henry, "The Fall and Rise of Strategic Planning," *Harvard Business Review,* January–February 1994.

Mohrman, Susan, Susan Cohen, and Allan Mohrman, Jr., *Designing Team-Based Organizations,* Jossey-Bass Publishers, San Francisco, California, 1995.

Nohria, Thomas, and Nitia Nohria, "Case Management and the Integration of Labor," *Sloan Management Review,* Winter 1994, pp. 11–21.

Office of the President, Office of Management and Budget, *Standard Industrial Classification Manual,* Executive Office of Management and Budget, Washington, D.C., 1987.

Osborne, David, and Ted Gaebler, *Reinventing Government,* Addison-Wesley, Reading, Massachusetts, 1992.

Pfeffer, Jeffrey, *Competitive Advantage Through People,* Harvard Business School Press, Boston, Massachusetts, 1994.

Ramcharamdas, Ennala, "Xerox Creates a Continuous Learning Environment for Business Transformation," *Planning Review,* March–April 1994.

Richter, Marsha, "Technology Acquisition and Implementation: Learning the Hard Way," *Government Finance Review,* February 1996.

Saxenian, AnnaLee, *Regional Advantage: Culture and Competition in Silicon Valley and Route 128,* Harvard University Press, Cambridge, Massachusetts, 1994.

Strebel, Paul, "Why Do Employees Resist Change," *Harvard Business Review,* May–June 1996.

U.S. Congress, Office of Technology Assessment, *State of the States Brownfields: Programs for Cleanup and Reuse of Contaminated Sites,* Office of Technology Assessment, OTA-BP-ETI-153, Washington, D.C., June 1995.

U.S. General Accounting Office, *Pay for Performance: State and International Public Sector Pay-for-Performance Systems,* GAO/GGD-91-1, Washington, D.C., October 1990.

U.S. Office of Personnel Management, *Broad-Banding in the Federal Government,* OS93-1, Washington, D.C., February 1993.

The Warner Group, *Citywide Organizational Assessment for the City of Glendale,* Woodland Hills, California, March 1994.

Zellman, Gail L., Joanna Zorn Heilbrunn, Conrad Schmidt, and Carl Builder, "Implementing Policy Changes in Large Organizations," in National Defense Research Institute, *Sexual Orientation and U.S. Military Personnel: Options and Assessment,* RAND, MR-323-OSD, 1993.